BECAUSE
WE
MUST

BECAUSE
WE
MUST

A MEMOIR

TRACY YOUNGBLOM

UNIVERSITY OF MASSACHUSETTS PRESS
Amherst and Boston

ISBN 978-1-62534-852-4 (paper)

Designed by Sally Nichols
Set in Freight Text Pro
Printed and bound by Books International, Inc.

Cover design by adam b. bohannon
Cover photographer unknown, *Light and Shadow,* courtesy Pxfuel.

Library of Congress Cataloging-in-Publication Data
A catalog record for this book is available from the Library of Congress.

British Library Cataloguing-in-Publication Data
A catalog record for this book is available from the British Library.

For Elias

For all our companions on the journey

CONTENTS

CONTENTS

BECAUSE
WE
MUST

NOT THE BOOK

No, no. No.

My twenty-three-year-old son, Elias, the youngest of my three boys, had just asked me a simple question, and I had responded viscerally, my words escaping without will or intention. This scene had unfolded while he was sitting in his wheelchair (temporarily, I hoped) at Regency Long-Term Care Hospital in Golden Valley, Minnesota, and while he and I were passing the time between his physical and occupational therapy sessions. His jaw was wired shut, and he was speaking around his trach tube that day, a trick he had recently taught himself.

The trach tube (a plastic protuberance, one end impaling his throat and another blunt end sticking out into plain air) allowed outside air to be drawn into his lungs with minimal effort. The tube was an upgrade; just a couple of weeks prior, a ventilator had breathed for him.

He was animated that day, though he appeared frail and encumbered. He and I had been chatting nonchalantly—as nonchalantly as we could, given the circumstances—when he had blurted out his question:

Are you going to write a book about me?

It had been a tough winter. Now, in late April, spring was finally erupting, offering hope. At home in my gardens, hosta and astilbe were knifing their green way through crusted soil (though I was rarely at home to see it). Elias had recently been interviewed by a couple of news reporters about his accident, so he was giddy. Just over a month into recovery, his progress was impressive: his physical wounds were healing; his bones were knitting together; his bruises were fading; his stitched abrasions were healing. He had moved, after three weeks in the ICU, to this transitional facility. We all—his family and friends—could see that he would return to his former physical self, mostly.

But his question jolted me out of my hard-won sense of stability, forced me back momentarily to confront the magnitude of his situation. That's why I responded so vehemently, instinctually refusing his suggestion. I wanted—I thought—to avoid capitalizing on his experience by writing about it. I hated the thought of drawing attention to myself when he had been the rightful focus of many people's thoughts for the past month. Yet he had a message I could help spread: *Don't let another person determine your life for you. Don't feel sorry for yourself.*

Moreover, I was—I am—a writer. Probably that is why Elias asked me the question in the first place. He knew that I often sift meaning from my experience by shaping it into poems, stories, and essays. In that sense, I ought to have seen his question as natural, but it was not one I had anticipated.

Partly, my surprise was due to lingering shock: the accident had been a fluke. He had simply been in the wrong place at the wrong time. Then there was the fact that, so far, his story had been unfolding in a way that was at odds with traditional, meaning-making narrative. The core of it made no sense. I didn't think writing about it could change that; I couldn't imagine offering any helpful perspective.

We continued to talk that day, and I moved past my initial shock to the next phase: hedging and feinting.

I don't want to use you to gain fame and fortune.

We both laughed at my comment, and then we joked about how we'd appear on *Oprah* together, about who would play him in the movie version.

Besides, I added, more seriously, *I don't know how your story is going to end. I can't write it until I know.*

I knew a lot. Elias's life was irrevocably altered, yet here he was, calm and far from vindictive. When I said I didn't know how his story was going to end, I meant I would hold out hope for better prospects until the end.

I know more now, several years later, about why I hesitated that day. Because this is *not* the book I intended to write. I had written prose before—reams of it—and in the back of my mind had planned to gather those essays someday into a book about the complicated entanglements of family and parenting and romantic relationships—subjects common to everyone, subjects I understood from experience. What I wrote about challenged me, but it didn't threaten to undo me. I could easily process it through writing.

In truth, I know nothing about living through a disaster like this. Elias's accident and its aftermath have left me short of patience, understanding, words. I have been—I remain—angry that I have this story to tell. Anger makes me want to resist the telling. However, I also go more regularly to the computer, strike keys, and compose sentences that, in their unspooling, show a way forward.

In attempting to write about it, I am learning how to write about it. Like Gerda in the film *The Danish Girl,* I seem to be—painfully, gradually, and somewhat unwillingly—discovering my subject.

That subject begins with our basic story.

On Monday, March 16, 2015, Elias was driving from Fargo, North Dakota, toward our home in Coon Rapids, Minnesota. He was fresh from a weekend visit to Fargo, where he was a student at North Dakota State University (NDSU).

He had been living with us—me and my husband Tim—since Christmas 2014, devoting his time to required teaching observations for his music education degree, plus working full time at Target and part time with the Blaine High School marching band (where he had been on staff since 2009). In addition, he went to the gym to lift weights four or five times a week.

Each moment of each of his days was consumed with the effort of laying the track for his future: he would finish his degree and student-teach by Christmas, fulfilling his goal of becoming a high school band director, embodying the ideals of those he had come to admire, men and women who had taught him how to read music and scores, to form a group out of disparate members, to exert effort, especially when he didn't feel like trying.

His chosen path was no surprise to me, no random decision. Ever since middle school, his life had been consumed by music. He had learned to play trumpet in band class in sixth grade; then later he had taught himself percussion. That adventure had led to an obsession with high school drum line and marching band.

The first time I'd heard him say *drum line,* he was pressuring me to sign a permission slip and write a check so he could join this afterschool activity. I had no idea what he was talking about, but I signed the form anyway, happy that he wanted to be involved. As I watched, I learned; he became slowly absorbed in that world of sound and rhythm, where music and choreography joined hands in an intricate dance—like marching band, but with only percussion instruments. He played cymbals his first year, then progressed to tenor drums and finally snares. During his junior year, his school's drum line won first place at the state tournament. Participating in this group had added layers of significance to his life.

Music had always kept him in school; though intelligent—gifted, even—he was not academically diligent. (I mean, of course, that he was lazy.) Music made his required math and English classes bearable. There was really no choice when it came time for college: his major would be music education.

Indeed, at two o'clock on that Monday afternoon in March, he was well on his way to his envisioned future. He was hurrying home, driving away from Fargo and toward an outing with a college friend to celebrate National Ice Cream Day. In the big-picture sense, he was also driving toward a level of success that we were all taking for granted; it was so certain that we didn't have to think twice about it.

But near Fergus Falls, about an hour east of Fargo, his plan was abruptly changed. Someone altered his plan, I mean. That someone—a driver—a forty-five-year-old woman—was drunk in the middle of the day and barreling the wrong way down the interstate. She collided with Elias's sturdy but compact Honda Civic. The resulting explosive collision sent it careening more than fifty yards into the ditch—it flipped several times on the way—while her Lincoln stalled, grunted, sat still in the median. Smoked.

I didn't find out about the accident until six o'clock that night because Elias's wallet and cellphone had been lost in the crash. Several days afterward, his dad and brothers went to visit the remains of the car and actually found his phone in the passenger-side door pocket. But they couldn't find his wallet. A state trooper returned to the accident scene several times after that, tramping through grass and swishing aside weeds in the field next to the freeway, trying to locate it. He never found it.

Because of that missing wallet and cellphone, no one could locate *me* the day of the accident. No one could communicate the trouble facing my son. When I finally found out about it—and the fact that my son had survived such a collision—I sprang into action.

A certain mental flexibility enabled me to drive carefully toward Fargo that night. Some part of me grasped the fact that focus was what I needed to arrive safely, so that I could hold his hand, reassure him, *I'm here, it's all right.*

I rehearsed that speech out loud in my car most of the way, talking to myself—talking to him—anticipating his response. When I entered his room, I believed he'd say, in his usual off-hand way, *Hi, Mama.*

When I stepped off the elevator at the hospital, my fantasy collided with reality. The nurse who met me, who talked nonstop all the way through the automatically swinging double doors of the ICU to his room, was trying to prepare me for my first sight of my son. Despite her efforts, I was not prepared.

Entering his room, I also entered a new world, one that was shrouded in the unfamiliar: medical specialists and surgeons, sedatives and transfusions, trach and feeding tubes, changes in medications, therapies and difficult diagnoses, long-term care facilities and rehab centers, and Lord knows what else. (I am still learning all the vocabulary his recovery necessitates.) But after that first night, though a stranger there, I made that new world my home. I live there now, in the land of recovery.

I still do not know how my son's story is going to end, but I know now that it is my story to tell, too—that I can tell my part of it. His progress has been steady, and I can gladly write about his remarkable spirit, his stamina, his refusal to give in to despair, because I have spent parts of nearly every day with him since the accident.

I have only gradually realized—and with hesitation—my part in this tale: my mother's perspective with its own landscape of recovery. I am a character in my son's story—as he is equally a character in mine.

This story—this book—was built of moments: of confusion, of anguish, of simple joy, of unexpected turns for the better or worse. The CaringBridge posts I composed for more than a year after the accident provided reminders and details of such moments as I wrote.

I decided when I began working on those updates, and eventually this book, that I would not mention the names of any specific medical personnel. I did not—I do not—want to single out anyone unfairly. The medical staff were, nearly without exception, the best in their fields, fully dedicated to my son and his progress: kind, hardworking, compassionate, inspiring.

Though I have written this story from my own perspective, other perspectives have influenced me. Like all dedicated English majors—and all avid readers—I have viewed my experience through the lens of other people's stories. I have naturally looked to poems and other writings when life became difficult to remind me that art can soothe and comfort.

One especially influential book was Abigail Thomas's memoir *What Comes Next and How to Like It,* a gift from a high school friend in the early days of Elias's recovery. While Elias was napping or sedated or working out with physical therapists at Regency Hospital, I plowed through my first reading of the book, camped in an orange vinyl hospital chair, not even registering its contents. At that time it was pure distraction. I have read it two or three times since then, so now I see what I missed the first time through: the beauty of telling a story in short bursts, of compiling a narrative out of fragments. Its interwoven reflections and subtle narrative arc mimic the way in which difficulties are processed: a bit at a time and not always directly. Thomas's book—all of my readings of it—helped me see a way to this book.

Elias has refused to define his life in terms of the accident. I have tried to adopt his optimistic approach. I have largely failed. But our journeys of recovery intertwine, running parallel and also diverging. What remains true for us—for me and for him—is this: we move forward, in our own ways, despite everything.

Because we must.

PART I

THE NEWS ARRIVES
ON FOOT

No matter how many times I recall the night of the accident—the surprise and shock of finding out, the numbness settling like fog—I relive it in the present tense. In my memory it is always happening again:

At six o'clock on a Monday evening, March 16, I hear a knock on my front door. I am not expecting any visitors.

How unusual, I think.

What an annoyance! I think.

I have been working at my computer, hurrying to finish preparations for the community education poetry class I will begin teaching on the following night—Tuesday, March 17, Saint Patrick's Day. It will be the first time I've offered this class, and it has twelve students registered, a strong enrollment for poetry.

My rushing is a prelude to more of the same. After I finish my final preparations, I must dash upstairs to change clothes for my 7:15 volleyball match. I realize I am cutting it close.

The knock persists. I linger at the keyboard, torn. The person may be someone running for office or trying to sell me siding—someone who will go away if ignored. But when the noise continues, I leave my computer grudgingly, stalk across the kitchen, and open my front door to a uniformed police officer standing on my front porch, his hands folded against his belt.

Can I come in?

Sure? My answer is almost a question.

Has a neighbor complained about me? Is there some city ordinance I've accidentally broken? Several years ago, a warning flyer had been left under the windshield wiper of Tim's car to announce that, in our neighborhood, parking directly across from another driveway was prohibited.

Are you the owner of a 2002 Honda Civic? the officer demands—but gently. I can't quite read his face. Is he trying to look official, or is he concerned?

Yes, I exhale. What does that have to do with anything?

Do you know who might have been driving that car?

I step back, haltingly, in dawning realization.

My son, I scratch out, suddenly aware I should have been expecting Elias from Fargo. He had said, vaguely, that he'd head for home this afternoon, but it was like him not to text or call, even if he were going to be late. He felt no obligation to keep me informed of his schedule, and I didn't expect it of him. That's why I hadn't been worried by his silence—until now.

The officer and I stare at each other.

There's been an accident, he says finally, lifting both hands, then letting them fall, a gesture that says, *I know it's not enough, but that's all I know.*

I don't respond—how am I supposed to respond? The news is delivered so passively. The officer thrusts a tiny slip of spiral notebook paper toward me. It hovers in the air until I grab it, peruse it, see that it is covered with handwriting.

That's the number of the state trooper who was on scene. You can call him for more information.

I still have that paper, its edges tangled in a messy fringe, like the frayed ends of an old rag rug.

I found out much later that this state trooper had been parked only a half-mile away from the accident scene, so he arrived within minutes of the crash to assess the damage and spring into action. I also discovered later that after he had acted quickly—secured an extraction crew as well as a helicopter transport to airlift my son to the nearest trauma hospital (in Fargo, from whence he'd come), interviewed witnesses and the two civilians who'd stopped to help, written his accident report, filled out a warrant for blood alcohol concentration for the other driver—he had also worked hard to track me down.

He'd Googled me. (He'd gotten my name from the insurance card in the car's glove compartment.) He'd called NDSU (apparently because Elias had said that he was a student there). He'd called Anoka-Ramsey, the college where I teach (information he'd found by Googling me). By that time—nearly five o'clock in the afternoon—no one was at the switchboard to answer the phone, verify my identity, and provide contact information.

Finally, out of desperation, he'd found my home address online (or maybe from the car's insurance policy card). Out of other options, he'd then contacted a local police officer and sent him to my house—this earnest and nervous young man now standing in front of me.

This odd way of finding out became an integral part of the story, the first of several revelations that arrived in an unexpected, unsettling way.

Now I grip the paper he's handed to me in shaking fingers—but not shaking so much that I am impolite.

Thank you, I say, noticing that my voice sounds strained, wavering. Foreign.

I set the paper down on the kitchen counter, smooth it flat, try to remain calm and steady. I grab my cellphone and prepare to dial, hesitating because this officer still stands in my entryway.

Would you like my contact information, too, in case you need anything from me later?

While he writes, I rock from foot to foot, still standing with my phone in my hand. The phone feels like a prop; our interaction feels like a scene in a bad movie. The officer hands me another slip of spiral notebook paper, this one scrawled with his name and phone number. This, too, I keep.

I want him to leave so I can make my call. But I don't want to be rude. He finally disappears, before or after I dial.

The state trooper answers his phone on the second ring, and I blurt out my only question: *Is he alive?* I assume he knows who I am. I may have introduced myself briefly, though I am not sure.

The news I hear from him I carefully transcribe, as if taking notes in a class (another paper I hang onto, all three folded and wedged into the checkbook inside my purse). As always, I write down what the expert says, not reacting, only recording: *Nearly head on. Wrong-way driver. Serious.*

I am so studious I don't even wonder why the other driver was going the wrong way down the interstate. Instead, listening intently, I write down exactly what he tells me: *facial fractures, head okay, liver mild, left arm, BP down, transfusion.* I squeeze in this information next to another list, one clearly meant for a trip to the grocery store: *turmeric, sesame seeds, ginger.* Under that, I scrawl *Phyllis* and the number of the emergency room or ICU—I'm not sure which. It's the next place I call for information.

Drive safely, the nurse (or whoever) exhorts when I pledge to be there as soon as I can.

I make two other essential phone calls after that: to Tim and to Elias's dad, Rich. Rich answers the phone right away and, after a quick conversation (*Yes, I'm going to drive there. I'm leaving in ten minutes*), I leave a detailed voicemail for Tim, who has a late meeting. Then I get down to business, running upstairs to pack quickly so I can start the journey to my son quickly.

While stuffing T-shirts and underwear into my backpack, I

suddenly and reflexively bend over, my arms crossing my belly. I gasp for breath—almost but not quite crying, more like heaving. This can't be the time for falling apart, I think, not the time for my body to betray my steadfast mind.

Pull yourself together, Tracy, I warn out loud.

Several deep breaths later, I straighten up, finish packing, watch myself assume a role: calm, decisive mother. I don't know what I will face when I get there, but I know who I must be—*The Impervious One. The One Who Can Handle Anything.*

How do I know? Because falling apart means my son could die.

WELCOME TO THE ICU
First Week

A strained, nervous energy propelled me to pack quickly and head west with no real idea of what I would encounter, and it kept me leaning forward in my car—literally and figuratively—in ignorant anticipation during the entire three-and-a-half-hour drive to Fargo. Yet the trip was surprisingly uneventful, and I arrived at the hospital at about 10:00 p.m. that Monday night.

As I'd started my vehicle and backed out of my driveway, I'd decided that I would travel west on Highway 10, with its multiple small-town slowdowns, rather than navigate the quicker default route of Interstate 94, with its semitrucks weaving from lane to lane at eighty miles an hour. This may have been a subconscious decision; some part of me knew I was not ready to pass the site of the collision—mile marker 56—even on the opposite side of the divided interstate. Deliberately choosing a route that avoided this direct confrontation helped convince me the trip would be easy.

I passed through many small towns on my drive: Royalton, Cushing, Verndale, New York Mills, Wadena. I noted their names, smiled at some of them—such curiosities—as if I were on a pleasure ride. I urged my car along and talked out loud to my son when the car became too silent: *I'll be there soon.*

I did take a gamble that night with my car's gas gauge—uncharacteristic for me—pushing through several towns after the gas light came on near Perham and eventually stopping to pump gas in Detroit Lakes. I was never panicked about running out of gas (though maybe I was panicked about something else), but I do recall considering the impossibility of it: could I actually run out of gas in the middle of this trip, on the way to visit my son in the hospital? *That could only happen in a bad movie*, I consoled myself.

Once I filled the tank, I drove the remaining forty miles to Fargo. I can't remember who gave me directions, or if anyone did, and I am generally not good at navigating, but I found the hospital easily. I parked in the garage and hustled up to Three East, the ICU.

The nurse who met me at the elevator and escorted me that night to Elias's room chattered all the way there. I did not stop to weigh the significance of his having a room in the ICU or a dedicated nurse. I vaguely remember her telling me, *He doesn't look very good right now.* Did she touch my arm as she spoke to me? I can't remember. I know I murmured in response to whatever muted warning she was giving.

The truth is that I couldn't imagine how badly my son was hurt or what that hurt might look like, no matter what she said, so I held onto that ignorance all the way to his door. The list of injuries I had copied down hours earlier had seemed neat and manageable; committing something to writing meant that it was ordinary. The list had made me believe *It's not that bad.* But once the nurse guided me to his room and I took in the full sight of him, the real story began.

His head was swollen to an unrecognizable size, a small watermelon. Both of his eyes were swollen shut: his eyelids bulged, red and purple, with bruising. Dark lines of stitches, along with bruises and cuts, crisscrossed both his arms and his face, including one crooked, deep gash on his left cheek that met his mustachioed upper lip, twisting it upward. Plastic tubes snaked around him. Three large striated ones had been shoved down his throat; his top and bottom lips were stretched as thin as crescent moons to accommodate the traffic. A thin one was implanted near his groin; another the same size pierced his right shoulder. His left arm was a bandaged mass, strangely akimbo, leaning against the bedrail. A rhythmic pumping—the ventilator, I would later learn—provided an eerie soundtrack.

My head swam in a dizzy whirl. I hardly registered the fact that Elias was not breathing on his own. My peripheral vision must've kicked in suddenly. I sensed that the silent nurse was nodding in sympathy, somewhere to my left, even as I began to buckle. She must have placed the chair behind me into which I collapsed, suddenly, without volition.

Later—perhaps within the first few hours—she explained to me the basics of my son's situation. He was being kept sedated and on pain medication and would be monitored carefully all night, his vitals checked constantly. She pointed out the red-lit console near his bed that flashed updates of his condition: blood pressure, heart rate. No one told me, that night, the specifics of what had happened in the ER during the hours it had taken to save him. I wouldn't find out those details until several years later.

Much later I would tell visitors, friends, anyone who would listen: *What you see on TV hospital shows is fake. They don't even come close to showing how bad accident victims look.*

Within thirty minutes of my arrival, my son Nate and his new girlfriend arrived. His dad had called him (had I asked him to?), and Nate had decided immediately to make the drive. He was tall—more than six feet—and tough—a National Guard soldier who had recently spent a year in Iraq. He was also especially protective of his younger brother.

I was in the family waiting area when they got there, and I walked with Nate into Elias's room and stood with my arm wrapped around his waist as he took in the first sight of his wounded brother. I remember gripping a belt loop on the waistband of his jeans, feeling his lean strength, and trying to absorb his grief: *Please, let me help him bear this.*

I felt his body tense in anger, then felt rather than saw him turn on his heel and stalk out of the room, hunched and mumbling.

An hour and a half after that, my oldest son, Caleb, arrived with Elias's dad and stepmom—Rich and Kay. I led Caleb in and stood beside him, intent on steadying him in a similar way. He was, at six foot four, the tallest of my boys; and as I leaned into him, I felt dwarfed and helpless. I couldn't read his face. What did I expect? He had always been reticent, outwardly calm, his thoughts beyond my comprehension. I had known, from the time he was a child, that he was a deep thinker, a reserved and solid presence. He stood silently next to me, taking in the situation, giving no hint of what might be swirling in his mind.

For the next several hours, all of us flowed in and out of room 308, our eyes scanning the various monitors for news. Elias's body was draped with a heavy warming blanket to raise his core body temperature, which had dipped due to the units of blood he had received earlier. The nurse explained, briefly, that units of blood were kept chilled, so transfusing them into a person always lowered their core temperature. Little of him was visible, but we held his good right hand or forearm and talked to him, in case he could hear us, while we waited for his body to rebound.

We could absorb a few bits of knowledge that first night, even in our distracted states. We watched his numbers—his blood pressure and core temperature rising in minute increments—reporting to each other on our return to the family waiting area, *It's up to 95.6, ,* almost gleefully. Despite the seriousness of the situation, we chatted, buoyed by each other's presence and by the factual confirmation of Elias's slowly rising vitals. There is a sort of joy in company when tragedy is near. We were not exactly happy that night, but we were elevated by each other. That we were all there, together, kept our worst thoughts at bay.

Someone—Elias's girlfriend, I think—suggested I start a CaringBridge site to keep people updated. That way, she said, I wouldn't have to worry about returning individual phone calls or answering emails. So sometime around one o'clock that first night, I created an account on the laptop I'd thought to shove in my backpack, and I wrote the first update, which was relatively brief and to the point:

> *Elias was involved in a serious car accident today on his way home from a visit in Fargo. He was struck by a driver going the wrong way on 94 and sustained serious injuries. Basically: he has multiple fractures in his face and jaw, a compound fracture in his left arm, and some liver damage. He lost a lot of blood but has responded well to transfusions so far.*
>
> *The hospital staff has been incredible, stabilizing him. Right now, he is doing OK—this first night will be telling. But so far so good. His blood pressure is steady and climbing, his body temp is also on the way up, and as far as the docs can tell, he doesn't have any brain or spinal cord injuries.*
>
> *In the morning, he'll have another CT scan to make sure his brain is OK, and he will have a visit from some surgeons to see when they might start putting him back together. He has a breathing tube and is being kept heavily sedated, but we are talking to him and sending love his way.*
>
> *Already we are grateful for all the concern and prayers. Please keep sending them, and we'll keep posting updates here. No visitors except immediate family, but we'll let you know if that changes.*

Around three o'clock that night—really, the next day—Elias's nurse suggested—demanded—that we all get some sleep. She herded us from our various locations back to the family waiting area, then doled out blankets and thin pillows. She explained that there'd be plenty of time to observe him later. There'd be meetings with doctors in the morning; we'd want to be as fresh as possible for those.

Obeying her briskness, we curled up in that large room and blessedly dozed for a few hours. I remember slumping in my orange vinyl armchair, trying to find a comfortable position for my neck against the chair's back. I wedged the blanket in around me, feeling gradually warmer, but doubting I could ever relax enough to sleep. I did, though, at least for a few minutes at a time. When I was not resting, I was scanning the room in the dim light, hoping to confirm that everyone else, at least, was getting some rest.

When Tuesday morning dawned, the first news from the head trauma doctor, at about 7:30 a.m., was good: another CT scan had confirmed that Elias had no brain or spinal cord injuries. We did a large-group double take; this outcome seemed miraculous. The doctors shared our sense of disbelief. *A head-on collision at seventy miles per hour and no brain injury?*

The head trauma doctor outlined the treatment plan, given the surprising results of early tests. They would keep Elias sedated and on pain medication until he was stable enough to begin the series of necessary surgeries to repair his broken bones: left arm first, then the myriad facial fractures. (Every bone below his eye sockets was broken.)

Propofol and fentanyl, the names of the main drugs used to sedate and numb him, slid easily into our vocabularies. No one said—and we didn't let ourselves imagine—that there was a chance he wouldn't make it.

Time moved in a surreal way on that first full day. We were able to contact the outside world, or it reached out to us. The most notable contact, albeit an indirect one, took place when the mother of Elias's former roommate sent a cooler of food because she didn't want us to leave the ICU to eat. We never saw her, but we felt her presence in this simple, profound gesture.

In between brief visits to Elias's room, we munched on the carrots, ham sandwiches, Triscuits, and grapes that Ben's mom had provided. Our group at this time still numbered seven: me, Rich and Kay, Nate and his girlfriend, Caleb, and Elias's girlfriend. We were easily the biggest support group in the family waiting areas. We noted this with some pride and some guilt, even as we struck up conversations with other families who were awaiting news, good or bad. We had the means to be there; not everyone had that privilege.

At about dinnertime on that first full day, a nurse told us that she'd lowered Elias's level of propofol, his sedative, and during that interval he had wiggled the fingers on his good hand and given a thumb's up when she asked him to. We were sorry to have missed it, but by that time there was other good news: the surgery to repair the compound fracture in his left arm was scheduled for that evening.

We could not fully absorb how quickly the staff was able to move into action. We were still stuck in jaws-open mode, aghast, in stasis. We had no concept of how long we'd been alert with no real sleep to revive us. We were bogged down by exhaustion, almost immobile. That the doctors were looking ahead felt both miraculous and disarming.

Shaking off our lethargy, we parents decided to get hotel rooms, booking them online at a Days Inn close to the hospital. Caleb and Nate could stay with us for at least one night as each room had two beds. We booked the rooms for Tuesday, reserving only a few nights initially, because we believed we would all be home soon, that we would not need more than a few nights' lodging.

As it turned out, we didn't get to our hotel rooms that Tuesday night. The surgery to repair the compound fracture in

Elias's left arm kept getting pushed back. He was finally wheeled into surgery after 11 p.m.

We understood, then, in a way we couldn't have before, what a great hospital he was in. All of the urgent cases from a broad surrounding area were brought to this trauma center for treatment, so surgery hours stretched around the clock. Any immediate trauma was dealt with first, and other scheduled surgeries were eased in around them, no matter what time of day or night. Because Elias had been stabilized, surgery could wait if other cases took priority.

We spent more hours intermittently napping in chairs—reclining ones, this time—in the surgery waiting area, watching for Elias's name on the TV monitors that showed patients' progress. First, it appeared in the list of those awaiting surgery, then in the list of patients undergoing surgery, finally in the list of those who were post-surgery.

We spoke briefly to the surgeon afterward. It was the middle of the night, and we had to shield our eyes from the overhead fluorescent lights, but we happily took in the news that everything had gone well. We straggled to our hotel rooms at about 3 a.m.—now Wednesday morning, March 18—for a few hours' rest. The good news was clear: Elias's broken arm had been set, a first repair and the start of a return to normal, we believed.

On Wednesday morning, when we returned to the hospital, the surgeon showed us the before and after X rays. We could see Elias's left-arm compound fracture on one X ray and the bones back in place on another, which showed a couple of lengths of hardware that appeared as dark dashes holding them steady. The only problem, the surgeon said, was that Elias had too much forearm muscle to close all the incisions properly.

What an interesting problem to have! We would never give Elias a hard time about going to the gym again.

During the surgery, the doctor said, he'd also removed gauze packing in and around Elias's cheeks and jaw as well as the multiple intubation tubes stuck down his throat. And he'd performed a tracheotomy. Our son now had a trach tube, inserted through a small slit in his throat, to which ventilator tubing attached.

He still wasn't breathing on his own—a crucial fact we didn't fully comprehend—but with much of the facial packing removed, he looked less puffy and more like himself. We had the impression that he was improving at astounding rates (even after a short day and a half) because we saw him so often and were noticing minute changes in his appearance. He was starting to look normal, though of course nothing was normal: nurses squeezed liquid protein into a feeding tube protruding from his stomach, and he couldn't open his eyes to see that we were there.

But when my sister Terri arrived later on Wednesday morning, she had a different reaction. I was not in the family waiting area when she got there, so she told me about her experience that evening, when she and I shared my hotel room.

Terri had told the nursing staff in the ICU that she was there to visit her nephew, so a nurse had directed her to Elias's room. She had walked in and then, confused, had walked immediately back out and said to the nurse lingering in the hallway, *No. I am looking for my nephew, Elias Youngblom.*

The nurse was bewildered. She had led Terri to the right room. But my son was so beat up that his own aunt didn't recognize him.

Caleb and Nate left late on Wednesday afternoon, returning to their essential jobs. As I hugged them goodbye, I pressed gas gift cards into their hands, generous offerings from friends and family members who had stopped by to keep us company. One, the dad of a high school friend of Elias's, explained that he thought we'd be doing a lot of traveling back and forth between Fargo and home so we could use some help paying for gas. Others brought prayers and companionship and a quality pillow for me so I wouldn't have to use the flat hotel ones.

The rest of the week sped by for those of us who remained in Fargo. The main event included a series of breathing trials to wean Elias off his reliance on the ventilator. Most of the time, heavily sedated and on pain meds, he couldn't interact with us. But sometimes his nurses would lower his level of sedation meds, and his respiratory therapists would turn off the ventilator. Then the alertness he gained from the lower levels of sedation would force him to breathe on his own and become more aware of his surroundings.

There were rough moments in those early trials. Elias would sometimes become agitated, cough and cry. But there were triumphs as well. On Thursday, March 19, just three days after the accident, Rich, Kay, and I entered his room during a breathing trial, and he opened his eyes and seemed to look directly at us. We believed at the time that he recognized us, heard our words of greeting, and was comforted by them. At the nurse's direction, he wiggled his fingers and toes and squeezed our hands repeatedly. Because this was the first time we had seen him respond to verbal cues, his simple actions left us in joyful tears.

There were other challenges as well. One morning, when I entered his room, a nurse was standing at his side, so I had to wait by his feet. I laid one hand on each instep in greeting. The simple gesture produced a flood of memory: I had not touched his feet this tenderly since he was an infant and every part of him was treasure. But I noticed that one foot was ice cold, the other hot. It was a small detail, but it sent me into a spiral of concern. I told the nurse, who was unfazed: *It's nothing.*

But I stayed by his feet all day, continuing to lay my hands on them. He was so deep in his own world, traveling to places we could not know. This was how I could reach him. I wanted to see if he had anything else to say.

On Sunday, March 22, almost a full week post-accident, as we parents were approaching Elias's room, we heard the telltale rhythmic beeps that signal *emergency* in the ICU. We assumed that another patient was in trouble. We had heard those beeps for a week running, and we had also witnessed dead patients being wheeled out, covered in heavy drapes. But when we entered Elias's room, we saw that the beeps were for him. He was trying to claw his way out of bed. He had swung both of his legs off the left side and was straining to reach his feet to the floor, gripping the mattress with his good right hand for leverage. It took a couple of nurses and all of the parents to uncurl the iron grip of his good hand and get him to lie back down.

After we coaxed him to resettle, we told him that we were proud of his fighting spirit. We believed that he was reacting to a situation he was fully aware of, simply trying to get himself out of the hospital. After all, he had become gradually more alert, more interactive. Though he couldn't talk to us, we knew he could open his eyes, cooperate with medical staff, and hear our words, responding sometimes with a grin or a nod.

By the end of the first week we were fatigued, giddy with relief, flooded with a barrage of emotions, but we knew one thing for certain: being with him in his recovery was a privilege, though it was painful.

We couldn't see very far ahead—who can?—and we weren't yet looking behind at the cause of all this torment; there would be time to do that later. So we centered ourselves in the knowledge that, though we hadn't chosen this path for our son, we had been chosen to be part of it. We would simply exist in it, be wholly present for his benefit and ours.

A REGULAR ROOM

One of the great gifts of Elias's time in the ICU was that Rich and Kay and I got to spend time together. Rich and I had divorced in 1995, and he and Kay had married in 2003; both of those events were now ancient history. Rich and I had always been cordial co-parents, maintaining a safe, amiable, coordinated distance, even when we weren't getting along personally. We made important decisions together, and he worked hard to continue and deepen his relationships with the boys, taking them to Norway in the summer of 2001 to visit his brother and camping and cooking with them on their frequent weekend visits.

Perhaps because of this history, we were able to support each other naturally at the hospital, laughing and crying and cajoling. But in this concentrated time, we also became friends again. We ate lunch together and spoke easily in between, drawn together by the tragedy of the accident and by our shared relief at our son's survival. We were grateful that we could be together without awkwardness. We could share our grief and support our son, take turns holding his hand, speaking words of encouragement to him, vocally guiding him toward healing. We drew closer as we adjusted to the magnitude of the accident, which was becoming clear as days bled into weeks.

At one point, I told Rich about the film *The Theory of Everything*, which I had seen when it came out. In one scene, Stephen Hawking and his ex-wife are at an event in his honor; they are talking, watching their children play, and he says to her, "Look what we made." Blessedly, that's how we were with each other.

We missed each other's families, even after twenty years, so we swapped updates about marriages, deaths, divorces, engagements, and notable accomplishments. We also speculated on Elias's future, articulating questions that, alone, we were afraid to ask. Would he be able to pursue a career in teaching? Would his current girlfriend stay with him or bolt? We couldn't fully envision his future, but Rich, Kay, and I peered together down that dim road, and we hoped.

During the second week in the ICU, Elias's condition continued to improve quickly and surely. We also had contact with people we hadn't expected to meet. On or about March 23, just one full week post-accident, Rich spoke to an eyewitness, a driver who had been traveling westbound on Interstate 94, parallel with the wrong-way drunk driver but on the other side of the divided highway. This man had seen the danger—the car careening the wrong way down the freeway—and he had opened his window, waved his arms, yelled across the grassy roadway median, trying to get the driver's attention so she would pull over, stop her perilous trajectory. He had witnessed the crash, then had reversed direction at the first exit and sped back down the eastbound lanes until he was close enough to hop out of his car and offer help.

We also had visits from a firefighter who had helped extract Elias from the car and from the state trooper who had saved Elias's life by ordering a helicopter transport—the same trooper I had called on the night of the accident. He looked as vulnerable and young as my son. (*No wonder he seems shell-shocked*, I thought.) The paramedic and the nurse who had been attendants on the helicopter transport to Sanford Medical Center's emergency room also came to check in.

The helicopter crew told us that Elias had remained conscious all the way to the hospital, able to squeeze his eyelids shut on command and to squeeze the nurse's fingers periodically (*every three seconds*, she'd advised). Though they related these facts straightforwardly, their eyes were wet as they observed him in bed with stable vitals instead of bleeding out in their helicopter.

The surgery to repair the fractures in Elias's face and jaw was scheduled for Tuesday, March 24, just a week and a day after the accident. Every bone in his face below his forehead had been broken, including the tiny ones around his eyes; *orbital* was the term we learned. His jaw alone had been broken in three places.

We understood the miracle of his situation—his luck. If his frontal (forehead) bone had been broken, we would have been facing a different scenario. His brain would surely have been injured, leaving us with an Elias different from the one we were so grateful to have, the one we knew.

The surgeon-specialist showed us a CT scan of Elias's broken bones and explained what he was going to do. He thought the operation would take about nine hours, so we hunkered down in the surgery waiting area again. But once the procedure started, the surgeon discovered that Elias's upper palate was more stable than he'd anticipated, allowing him to avoid some riskier incisions. Midway through the procedure, he came out to personally update us with this news. He had wired Elias's jaw shut to stabilize it, he said, but those wires would stay in place for only three weeks instead of the six he had predicted initially. When he showed us the CT scan taken post-surgery, we could see that the minute cracks in the orbital bones had been mended.

Still, there was one bone on the outer side of Elias's right eye that the surgeon hadn't been able to position to his liking. So a few days after the surgery, when the swelling had gone down, he made sure Elias had enough medication for pain and then carefully pressed his fingers on the bulge from the outside, moving it into place.

The ventilator trials began to go steadily well during the second week in the ICU, and when Elias was breathing on his own, he became more responsive—and at other times, too. Examining his eyes post-surgery, the surgeon asked Elias if he could see, and he nodded. He smiled on command, to show the surgeon that his facial nerves were working. One day when the surgeon asked him to pucker up, our son hunched his shoulders, crinkled his eyes, and vibrated. He couldn't open his mouth, could barely open his eyes, but he was laughing.

All of this good news was intoxicating. We believed our son was a super-patient; we expected him to continue to defy expectations. We started to envision the upcoming Easter holiday, all of us celebrating together at home.

Elias also began to interact more, even providing answers to some questions, though he couldn't yet speak. When I asked how he was feeling, he raised his eyebrows in a kind of smirk that meant either *so-so* or *how do you think I feel?* When Rich told him that he was still in Fargo, he raised them again in a look of surprise. We told him that, when the nurses had to suction his lungs or change dressings, it would hurt but assured him that they were only trying to help. He nodded with understanding, we were sure. When the nurses asked him if he were in pain, he could signal yes or no.

Both Rich and Kay had to return home periodically for work, so one or the other was sometimes gone. In their absence, other family members came to fill in and keep Elias company: Rich's sister, my mother.

I was more fortunate than Rich and Kay were. My dean had arranged for substitutes to teach my classes so I could remain in Fargo. I stayed connected with these generous colleagues by sending instructions and documents via email every night from my hotel, which left me free to concentrate fully on Elias's recovery during the day.

We formed a stable, though varying, group. No one had to navigate Elias's recovery alone. All of us, together, comprised a revolving cadre of hardcore cheerleaders, dedicated to encouraging our boy on to recovery.

Whoever was in attendance went back and forth from the hospital to the hotel, our days developing a comforting rhythm. We'd arrive at the hospital at 7:30 or 8 a.m. We'd take turns going in and out of Elias's room to check on him; we'd hold his hand or rub his arm. Parents would sign consent forms for the many surgeries and procedures he underwent. We would walk to the cafeteria for lunch, where we'd chat with nurses about his progress, the size of his pupils, the way his body was accepting nourishment through his feeding tube. When we returned to his bedside, we'd speak with doctors about a timeline for moving him out of the ICU. After all of this activity, we'd return to our hotel rooms at about 8 p.m., after the 7:30 shift change delivered a nurse we hoped we already knew so that Elias could have the benefit of a familiar presence when we weren't there.

Very little of this was frightening or alarming. We were glad to have the intensive care of the nurses and grateful for the company we shared. Elias was rarely alone in his room, except overnight. Each ICU nurse had only two patients, so someone was there with him for at least half of the night, too.

During this time, Elias tolerated deep suctioning of his lungs (to prevent pneumonia), a procedure that seemed to draw the life out of his body from the inside. During these moments he reached out his hands to us, held on tightly. He communicated as well as he could: with raised eyebrows, nods, gestures. For a while, he was making a motion with his right hand as if he were throwing a baseball, an odd gesture we never fully understood.

He endured breathing trials off the ventilator, often vomiting or struggling in response, but sometimes lying still, untroubled.

Staring at our son, who was doing nothing except breathing, was deeply peaceful, like watching an infant curl and uncurl its fingers, a gesture almost unnoticeable to anyone but parents, to whom it is noteworthy, a thrill and a delight. The Sanford ICU nursing care was superb, each small thoughtful gesture spiking our hope and gratitude.

One nurse took the time to clean Elias and wash his hair, combing it over into a pompadour. She preferred her patients to look good, she said. She also confided to me that, in her many years as a nurse, driving to and from her shifts, she had seen drunk drivers on the road at all hours of the day and night. (*Even in the morning?* I asked naïvely.)

Another night nurse, realizing that Elias was frustrated because he couldn't talk, worked out a system with him. If he wanted something, he would tap on the bedrails twice with his left-arm cast to get her attention. She also figured out that his frustration was partly due to the way he was sliding down on the slippery hospital mattress, which was kept elevated because of his facial swelling and the ventilator. She shortened his bed so that his feet could rest against the footboard, and he could push himself up on his own. This was a remarkable feat of ingenuity, a palpable blessing.

On Saturday, March 28, less than two weeks after the accident (and, coincidentally, my birthday), we experienced a remarkable day of progress. One respiratory therapist, in response to a less-than-perfect breathing trial that morning, suggested inserting an O-ring, a new piece of equipment. The O-ring was a piece of plastic tubing, maybe three inches long and three-quarters of an inch in diameter, that would slide onto the trach tube slit in Elias's throat and open to the outside. She said that Elias would be able to breathe through it and cough up any secretions through it as well, unattached from the ventilator's long length of tubing. It was the tubing that was causing the problem, she explained. It penetrated deep into his lungs, so it was hard for him to relax and breathe when the ventilator was turned off because the tubing was rattling inside him as his lungs expanded with air.

I was skeptical. Elias was having a hard enough time as it was, and I didn't want him to undergo any experiments that would make things worse for him. Still, we agreed to try; and when we returned to the room after the procedure, we saw our son sitting up in bed, calmly breathing. He spent the whole of that momentous Saturday sitting up, breathing through the O-ring, and entertaining his visitors: Tim, his brothers, his grandparents, my sisters and their husbands, his best friend Jared. He freely distributed fist bumps, pumped his own right fist, gestured, nodded, and expressed himself more than we'd seen him do for two weeks. He was doing so well that Tim and I felt able to leave the hospital for a steak dinner with my parents to celebrate my birthday.

This mountaintop experience was followed, unfortunately, by a two-day period of delirium, a common pattern for trauma patients. It was painful for everyone. Elias thrashed around in his bed for almost twenty-four hours, never still for more than a minute. He didn't recognize us. Worse, he couldn't respond, though he had been reactive just a day earlier. One morning when I came in, I discovered he had torn out the IV from the back of his hand; the needle hung limp, and there was a skid of blood across his skin. In addition, his pupils were constantly dilated, probably from the heavy narcotic painkillers. The doctors, in response, changed his medication, adding an antipsychotic drug (a change that concerned me) in hopes of bringing him out of his delirium.

Even this period of uncertainty didn't dampen our spirits. It was a setback, but it had to be a minor one. As Elias came out of the delirium, he began to respond again, answering nurses' questions: *Are you comfortable? Are you in pain?* He performed familiar gestures that caused us to marvel—right hand rubbing his forehead or scratching at his sweaty long hair. He picked up his bandaged left arm to move it, motioned to us when he wanted to hold our hands, curled his legs or stretched them out to push at the foot of the bed. He twisted, he turned, he leaned, he rolled. His eyebrows alone told the story of his day, rising in skepticism or doubt or pain or confusion.

By Wednesday night, April 1—the middle of his third week in the ICU—he was suddenly back, returned to us. He sat up, alert, and played an elaborate game of charades, jerking his thumb toward his chest (so we thought), pointing to his wrist (*Watch?* we said, and he nodded), then pointing at himself again.

As it turned out, he was better at the game than we were. It took intense effort to get us to understand his message: *Time Me Leave?* What he meant was *When do I get out of here?*

He had been fully off the ventilator since the insertion of the amazing O-ring, and doctors had announced that one more day would determine that he was officially off it for good. On Thursday morning, April 2, a surgical physician's assistant removed the cast on his left arm and replaced it with a splint. She showed him how to do range of motion exercises in bed to begin to rehabilitate his injured left arm. A physical therapist came the next day to work on his legs, helping him complete leg lifts and foot stretches in bed. By that afternoon, he was declared ready for a room on a regular floor, which had been the goal all along. Overflowing with joy, we helped move him and his few possessions to Three South.

Once he was settled, he kept gesturing to ask, *What time is it?* We took this as a sign that he was working hard on his recovery and would return home soon. He had less intensive nursing care in the regular room—one nurse on a regular floor was responsible for five or six patients—so we worked to make him comfortable. We stood on each side of his bed, grabbed his arms, and hauled his thinning body up when he slid down every fifteen minutes or so. I learned how to suction saliva out of his mouth, which pooled there because his jaw was wired shut, as he held my hand and guided the suctioning wand.

What a marvel our time at the hospital had seemed. *How could almost three weeks have gone by so fast*, we wondered, flooded with gratitude? *How could we have been so lucky as to have our son returned to us, whole?*

A SUDDEN DIFFERENT VIEW

On April 3—the Friday before Easter—Rich and I stood at either side of our son as a doctor moved a pen light back and forth in front of Elias's face, instructing him to follow the beam with his eyes. This exam was routine; many doctors had performed it over the past three weeks. But the scene had two new elements: we had spent the day settling Elias into his room on a regular floor of the hospital; and this doctor was unknown to us, not a familiar staff member from the ICU.

As the pen light moved, Elias remained still, upright in his chair—a third unsettling element that made me jittery, made my stomach lurch slightly. Was he joking around? Was he tired? Was he weary of the same exams repeated over and over?

Okay, the doctor said, repeating the motion for the second or third time. *Just move your eyes to follow the light. The rest of you can stay still.*

Our son did nothing in response. Finally, he shrugged his shoulders, lifting both of his hands and holding them like empty bowls.

Rich and I stared at each other. We didn't say anything to

Elias. There was some talk of a scan of his eyes. Later we started to rationalize the situation to each other because the slowly dawning truth was too stark to accept: *It's the narcotic drugs. His pupils are still too dilated to focus. He could see before, but now he can't. What does that even mean?*

Besides, we reasoned, *the ophthalmologist who examined him before his facial surgery said the eyes looked good.*

Can't we get another doctor? we wondered.

We were trying to ignore reality. But we were forced to admit that the day had been strange in many ways. Elias had had a kind of panic attack right after moving to his new room, the first such reaction we'd ever seen. His blood pressure had risen suddenly, and his whole body had started shaking. His nurse and I had physically held him, talked to him, calmed him down. Had this been a sign?

Rich and I made no announcements to any other family members. We had just moved Elias from the ICU, after all, a grand gesture of optimism. We needed some time to adjust to the new room and routine, and so did he. Probably his inability to see was just part of the transition.

Privately, we sensed that the floor had started to shift. Yet we still believed we could handle any news; we believed that on the next morning he would be able to see again. We kept up an incessant, unrepentant chatter—mostly internal—as we went back to the hotel. Rich and I could not accept that Elias couldn't see, especially given that no one had told us that this could become our new truth. Or maybe we had missed something?

By the next day—Saturday, April 4—many other family members had joined us, traveling to Fargo to celebrate Elias's progress, to see for themselves the miracle of his survival—my mom and stepdad, Nate and his girlfriend, my sister Terri and her daughter Tina. They were unaware of our new information, and we didn't know how to explain that something had changed (*had it?*).

In response to our general confusion and questions, the chief trauma doctor at Sanford had consulted an eye specialist at the University of Minnesota, and that afternoon he called a meeting of the entire family. Along with medical staff, we assembled in a conference room at about 2 p.m., separated from our son, who rested in his bed in a spacious room just down the hall.

We sat stiffly in our chairs, as if our posture could ward off the worst or our resistance make the story turn out differently. I remember automatically turning my head from side to side, like an oscillating fan, my eyes taking in the room.

The chief trauma doctor immediately framed the stark reality: *Your son's optic nerves are dead.* His explanation left us with questions but without room to maneuver.

Other doctors, smiling tightly, chimed in. They didn't know *how* Elias had lost his sight, though they offered some possibilities: severe swelling due to the trauma of the accident, the carotid embolization done in the ER to save his life, the surgery done to repair his facial fractures. They could only explain *what* had happened: when blood flow to the optic nerves is cut off, they die, but sight survives for a time, diminishing only gradually.

This is consistent with Elias's experience, they said.

The optic nerves are the only nerves in the body that can't regenerate, they said.

We asked questions, all of them beginning with *But can't you . . . ?* To each, they simply shook their heads.

We weren't looking for someone to blame. It didn't matter *why* he had lost his sight. We were only trying to figure out what to do next, how to sit with this sudden heavy truth—how not to collapse under it.

Rich and I decided to tell our son the news together because we feared it might spiral him into a darkness of spirit to match the new darkness of his world. We hoped we could prevent that somehow. We sat beside him and choked out some useless words—but he seemed to already know. He nodded, just barely.

To fill in the emptiness, we responded to his silence with chatter, falling into clichés, soft pillows to cushion our despair.

Maybe we can find a specialist.

We will be here for you, no matter what.

We looked into his face, his blank eyes—eyes we had been convinced could see us so recently. We probed his reactions. We held his hands. His jaw was still wired shut, so he couldn't speak. He seemed to sink further into the bed. Some tears slid toward his ears, but how could we know what they meant? They may have been caused by the eyedrops the nurses had insisted on squeezing in three times a day. I thought bitterly, *He hates those drops. Maybe they'll stop that now.*

Elias made no sound, and his silence was fitting: the air drained of words, as our words seemed drained of meaning.

Then the whole family got busy. We spent the rest of the afternoon and early evening calling anyone we knew who had a medical background. We Googled medical resources; we considered multiple plans. We discussed transferring Elias to the Mayo Clinic or to another specialty hospital, where doctors might be able to do something more or something different. The Sanford doctors had offered no new treatment plan, just a continuation of his current one: to recover generally from the accident. They advised us that no hospital would do anything different. As we called around, we discovered that they were right.

A sense of nervous urgency overtook me. I felt I couldn't afford to waste time, to stop or slow down. I brushed aside my weight of sadness as if it were crumbs on the counter. I tried to ignore a nagging, irrational anger—at Elias's optic nerves for not announcing their intention; at his eyes, which had offered the lie of sight without hinting that it would be fleeting.

Later that weekend, Rich stopped me in a hall of the hospital and stared hard at me.

Are you all right, Tracy? He paused. *You have to take care of yourself too.*

I'm fine, I smiled.

Yes, of course. I would always be fine.

I babbled something about knowing my own limits and walked away smiling, a perfect exit, stage left.

ARRANGEMENT

There were pineapple slices cut into stars, into pineapple flowers with neat, arced petals and cantaloupe-ball centers. There were melons—cantaloupe and honeydew—wedged into leaflike shapes with crinkle-cut edges, strawberries interspersed like fireworks, explosions of deep red in the yellow and green field. The arrangement was beautiful, deft. We couldn't see the apparatus that was holding the whole thing together, but we selected individual parts—even as we hated to interrupt its symmetry—and ate them, juice dripping down our chins. There was in the room nervous laughter, a stifled giggle or two.

It was Easter weekend, Saturday night, when Jesus had lain in his tomb, when all hope had drained from his followers.

A hotel is not really a hospitable place, but in one crammed room we tried to pretend otherwise: Nate and his girlfriend, my mom and stepdad, Rich and Kay, and later Tim, who had decided to make the long drive from his family's Easter celebration in Iowa to join us in Fargo. I can't remember who sent the edible arrangement nor in whose room we chose to gather. But I know we ate together (a communion not less joyful for its necessity), having skipped regular dinner after learning the truth about Elias's eyesight.

For three weeks, we'd been certain he had defied fate, certain the drunk driver had not been the instrument of his demise. But his survival was incomplete; suddenly it had become a miracle with a dash of bitterness.

After making our numb way back to the hotel, we sat in chairs and nibbled at the beautifully cut fruit. Our stomachs, like the rest of us, had hardened in response. This was the only food we could handle—so easy to pluck, bite, swallow. We could think of no other way to use our mouths.

Eventually we opened wine, flipped caps off beers, drank—slowly at first, then more confidently. Why not? Like those early followers of Jesus, we had no notion about what would come next. We could have gotten drunk on our misery alone. Its heaviness made us sway. We had become unmoored from our former consciousness of the world.

Yet even then we pursued hope. Our conversation turned a corner, iterating a shy faith we'd doubted we had. Or maybe it was the wine speaking.

He's going to be fine, someone said.

He's as stubborn as they come. We all agreed.

He won't let this slow him down. Look how far he's come already. How could anyone object?

The clichés kept us up and talking, long past a reasonable hour. What was reason to us? Elias's survival was a fact beyond reason; but now this troublesome, unexpected outcome had redefined reason. Reason had asserted, *I've got your back.* Now it seemed suspect. Traitorous.

Yet after a while we slept and woke, as reasonable people will do. We retraced our routes to the hospital the next day, reentered Elias's room with words of comfort and cheer, however rehearsed.

It was Easter Sunday. Instead of a miraculous, unforeseen

turn of events, a redefinition of our lives—a resurrection of sight—we faced the fact that Elias was still blind. He had not returned to some former idyllic state.

We breathed in and out, evidence of reality.

Amen.

RECOVERY IN TWO ACTS, WITH AN INTERLUDE

Elias
Mother/Narrator
Dad
Visitors
Therapists
Various physicians and hospital staff
Maisie the dog

ACT ONE:
SCENES FROM REGENCY

April 8, 2015: Elias is transferred from Sanford Medical Center in Fargo, North Dakota, to Regency Long-Term Care Hospital in Golden Valley, Minnesota. He no longer needs intensive care. He needs to move to phase 2: to a facility closer to home where he can regain strength and recover enough to transfer to a phase 3 facility, a place where he can learn to walk again and take care of himself.

Picture: a stage that's mostly dark, except for a spotlight that illuminates Elias in a hospital bed in the middle of that light. The head of his bed is raised.

Imagine: this is his world. It may be any time of day, but it is always dark to him. People can see him, but he can't see them.

As characters come and go, he remains bathed in light; everyone else remains only slightly visible, as moving shadows outside the bright light. Voices are audible, but human forms are hidden. It's hard to be sure who's moving around in the periphery of the light.

Characters must be identified by the audience by voice, as Elias is forced to identify them.

Time remains undefined, as it is for Elias.

Scene 1

Room at Regency Hospital. Dad fusses near the bed, arranging blankets, storing a bulky backpack.

ELIAS (*Strained*):
Where's my phone?

MOTHER/NARRATOR (*Entering*):
You're talking! How is that possible? Your jaw is wired shut and you have a trach tube.

DAD:
He figured it out in the ambulance on the way here.

ELIAS (*Patiently*):
Where's my phone?

MOTHER/NARRATOR:
I'm so happy you can talk to us!

ELIAS (*Now with strained patience*):
Where's my phone? When can I have a drink of water?

MOTHER/NARRATOR AND DAD:
We're not sure.

They settle into chairs placed on opposite sides of Elias's bed.

ELIAS:
What happened to the other driver?

Mother/Narrator stands, moves forward, turns to face audience.

MOTHER/NARRATOR:
I am all about words; I have made my livelihood of them for the past twenty years. Yet sometimes words are inadequate. That is why I haven't written a single poem since the accident. Words are all we have, but words seem woefully unfit.

Still—I can't deny they matter. For instance, words of encouragement and support—they are not insignificant. If you don't know us well and wonder if what you say will matter, I stand here and tell you: *please speak*. It matters to us.

If you do know us well and still struggle with what to say—we understand. There are no right words. The words that come to you are all the words you need.

Backs near the bed again, signifying it is another day.

How do you like the nursing staff here?

ELIAS:
They have a lot of patients. But they come running when you try to get out of bed.

MOTHER/NARRATOR:
What happened?

ELIAS:
I wanted something last night, but no one would come. So I leaned my body over the side of the bed, and the alarm started beeping (*pantomimes this motion as he speaks*). I almost fell out of bed. Finally, someone came.

A few days later. There are now gym mats by the side of the bed.

MOTHER/NARRATOR (*Looking around*):
Did you try to get out of bed again?

ELIAS:
Lots.

MOTHER/NARRATOR:
Why?

ELIAS:
Something to do.

A few days later. Same room.

When they cut the wires holding my jaw shut, can I sign out of this place?

MOTHER/NARRATOR:
They say you have to go to a rehab facility next.

ELIAS:
I want to go home.

MOTHER/NARRATOR:
I'm sorry, you can't go home yet. You still need therapy.

ELIAS:
Anything I would do in a rehab facility I could do at home.

Visitors enter at both sides, laughing in the shadows. Hands reach out and touch Elias, patting him on the shoulder or grabbing his hand and shaking it.

VISITOR:
Want a drink of water?

ELIAS:
Yes, please.

Visitor:
What do you do all day?

ELIAS:
Exercise in bed.

Visitor:
What kind of workout did you get today?

ELIAS:
Chest and legs.

VISITOR:
Goodbye! Good to see you! See you later.

ELIAS *(Chuckling to himself)*:
But I won't see you.
How are you?
How's your girlfriend?
What classes are you taking this semester?
Who's getting married?

Dad, this is Freak Show.
Grandma, can I have some ice chips?

Scene 2

Elias is still in the middle of the light. Now a wheelchair and a chair sit next to his bed, in the periphery of light.

MOTHER/NARRATOR (*To audience*):
Elias has now been in bed for four weeks. I know in my mind that when a person is immobile, their muscles atrophy. But the full reality didn't hit me until I saw him start moving around outside the bed.

A physical therapist enters, reaches into the light to support Elias as he sits up, then stands up next to his bed with effort. Then he sits down again, exhausted.

He stands again, assisted, walks slowly to the chair, sits down, then rises and walks back to the bed and sits. The light follows him as he moves.

ELIAS:
It makes me tired when it's dark all the time.

THERAPIST (*As she speaks, Elias does what she asks*):
Let's see if you can get to the chair without my help, with the walker. Good. Now back to the bed.

Now sit on the edge of the bed. See if you can raise your knees one by one, like you're marching.

Elias breaks into a sunny smile as he moves his bent legs up and down, reacting to the word marching. *Another therapist enters.*

THERAPIST:
How's Mr. Amazing? Maybe you'd like to go outside today?

ELIAS:
I can smell it—someone's grilling.
It's strange to feel the sun without being able to see it.
I've never really heard the birds before, but now I do.

Scene 3

North Memorial Hospital. Recovery room—a small room with just a bed. Elias has had the wires on his jaw cut so he can speak more freely.

A surgeon stands next to him, with Mother/Narrator *near. All of the stage lights are up.*

NURSE (*Entering*):
Here's some 7-Up. You must be thirsty from the procedure.

Elias drinks, smiles beatifically.

SURGEON:
Everything looks good. I prescribe a tonsillectomy diet—soft foods. I wrote it in the discharge paperwork (*handing papers to* Mother/Narrator). Good luck, young man.

Scene 4

Regency Hospital. Elias in bed, still bathed in light. A nurse is there; various visitors enter.

NURSE:
Someone from speech must come and clear him for solid food.

ELIAS (*To nurse*):
What do you mean I can't get anything to eat? I'm starved!

MOTHER/NARRATOR:
The doctor wrote orders for a soft-food diet. It's right there in the paperwork I just gave you.

NURSE (*Glancing cursorily through the paperwork*):
He'll have to wait until morning.

Visitors approach bed.

VISITORS:
We brought you a fruit smoothie.
We brought you a root-beer float, your favorite.

Elias drinks contentedly.
Several therapists enter, pantomime an elaborate ritual of spooning

food into his mouth. They exit, and a dietician enters with a tray.

ELIAS (*Chewing*):
Mashed potatoes! Scrambled eggs! Bread pudding!

Time passes.

Mac and cheese! Ice cream! Mountain Dew!

Nurse enters.

NURSE:
I'm sorry, but your trach can't be capped until tomorrow.

ELIAS:
More mashed potatoes!
I'm hungry, I'm thirsty, I'm hungry, I'm thirsty, I'm hungry, I'm thirsty.
I'm alive.

A COMIC INTERLUDE

For this scene, all the stage lights go up: everyone is visible: Elias is in his wheelchair and behind him are nurses, doctors, hospital staff, Mother/Narrator.

Everyone else, except Elias, performs a mock can-can and other wild dances, continuously.

As characters speak, they come forward to interact with Elias, then retreat to dance. Each doctor is a new, different doctor.

Mother/Narrator stands in the middle of the group, slowly turning in circles. She stops twirling whenever she speaks.

MOTHER/NARRATOR:
Here begins the saga of the mysterious left-foot pain, which bridges the stays at Regency Long-Term Care Hospital and Courage Kenny Rehabilitation Center.

Just days after beginning to walk and regain his strength, Elias suddenly develops a terrible pain in his left foot, seemingly unrelated to the accident.

In its own way, it is hilarious.

As practitioners come forward, everyone else remains in the background, dancing.

DOCTOR:
Let's get an X ray to rule out a stress fracture from the accident.

MOTHER/NARRATOR:
His left foot was not really involved in the accident.

DOCTOR:
Might be blood clots. Let's do an ultrasound.

ELIAS (*In obvious pain*):
When you scan near my groin, I can hardly stand it. It's got to be nerve pain.

DOCTOR:
While we're at it, let's increase his pain meds.

MOTHER/NARRATOR:
Let me try some Arnica on it—it's natural.

DOCTOR:
The X ray was clean, but since there are no blood clots, we'll X ray again.

DOCTOR:
I'm going to prescribe gabapentin for nerve pain. It's probably nerve pain.

MOTHER/NARRATOR:
Can't you try something natural?
Aside. This is a pain in the ass.

DOCTOR (*Peering at Elias*):
Are you depressed? You must be depressed. Let's try some antipsychotics.

ELIAS:
I'm not depressed.

DOCTOR:
I think we should try another X ray. And no more walking
until we get to the bottom of this.
If the X ray looks good, we'll do a CAT scan.

DOCTOR:
In the meantime, we'll do a nerve conduction study. And let's
increase the gabapentin.

DOCTOR:
We can see some blockage of the sciatic nerve. We need to do
an MRI of the lumbar spine.

ELIAS:
I told you it was nerve pain!

THERAPIST:
I used to be a massage therapist. Let me work that calf a
little.

DOCTOR:
I ordered a triple-phase bone scan; I want to see if it's complex regional pain syndrome. In the meantime, we ordered
this huge heavy sandal for him to wear when he stands or
walks.

Doctors begin to dance more slowly, and slowly they exit the stage.

MOTHER/NARRATOR (*To audience*):
It turned out to be complex regional pain syndrome, which
sounded like a made-up condition, except that a physical
therapist gave me an article to read about it. It happens when
a limb or extremity experiences pain out of proportion to
the severity of injury; nerves misfire and tell the brain that
even light pressure is excruciating. It's almost impossible to
diagnose and even more difficult to treat.

I am not sure, even now, how they can be sure this is the
cause of the mysterious left-foot pain.

DOCTOR:

I'm going to recommend a nerve block.

ELIAS:

Is it dangerous?

DOCTOR:

Well, the doctor will have had a lot of practice sticking a long
needle into your spine at precisely the right place.

It doesn't always work the first time; if that's the case,
you'll have to decide whether to try it again.

ELIAS:

Well, the first injection didn't help.

Physical therapy has accounted for all my progress so far.

No thanks, docs—joke's on you. I healed myself.

ACT TWO:
SCENES FROM COURAGE CENTER

Scene 1

*Elias sits center stage in a wheelchair. There is a bed slightly behind
him and off to one side. The light overall is brighter now but tapers
to shadow within about six feet of Elias on either side—his growing
adjustment.*

*This is his large room at Courage Center, the rehab facility where
he has been moved so he can ramp up his therapies and prepare for a
return home. Time passes and remains undefined. Family members
and staff enter and exit.*

DAD:

Here's your new room. It's huge. You get to wear your own
clothes now, brush your teeth with your own toothbrush.

ELIAS:

I hope the food is good.

DAD (*Wheeling Elias*):

There's a big private bathroom, too, with a huge shower.

Sound of running water.

ELIAS:

Ahhhhhhh . . . first shower in six weeks.

ELIAS (*Back in bed, to his cellphone*):

Call Mom.

MOTHER/NARRATOR:

Hi, honey, how was your first night?

ELIAS:

When are you going to get here?

MOTHER/NARRATOR:

I'm on my way.

ELIAS:

Silence. Sniffles. Muffled crying. Mother/Narrator approaches.

MOTHER/NARRATOR (*To audience*):

It sucks to be twenty-three and blind. The Regency staff did
everything for him. If he said he was too tired for therapy,
they let him nap. They brought him fans and blankets, gave
him extra fluids through the IV because he was thirsty.
It didn't matter that he was blind; he didn't have to face
it. Now everything is different. The goal here is rehab—
progress. This staff won't let him off the hook.

He'll have to buck up and do it.

*Nurses and Therapists enter individually, surrounding Elias and
talking in turn.*

THERAPIST:

Let's stretch that left calf.

THERAPIST:

Let's work on flexibility in your hand. Curl each finger to your palm, one at a time.

THERAPIST:

Here's your white cane. Wave it back and forth; use it to feel around the perimeter of the room. That's how you get your bearings.

NURSE:

You are still on a soft-food diet, but we're not giving you anything through the feeding tube overnight so that can come out soon.

ELIAS:

They wouldn't let me have a grilled ham-and-cheese sandwich in the cafeteria. They only let me eat rice. I wanted a grilled ham-and-cheese.

THERAPIST:

Let's try these sandals your mom brought. They should be more comfortable than squeezing into your sneakers. Pretty soon we'll get that wheelchair out of here.

Elias's room: Therapist and Mother/Narrator stand together.

THERAPIST:

You still have a pin in your hand. Is that from your surgery?

MOTHER/NARRATOR:

Yes. We aren't sure what to do about these leftovers from his stay in Fargo.

THERAPIST:

Once the pin is removed, Elias can do some therapy in the pool.

Mother/Narrator moves away from Elias; she is now outside the room, on the phone, leaving messages.

MOTHER/NARRATOR:

Hi, I'm Elias Youngblom's mom. Dr. ___ performed surgery on him in Fargo; I'm calling to see if we must drive to Fargo for the pin removal. Please call me back.

Hi, I'm calling to see if you have a hand specialist on staff. My son had surgery on his arm and hand, and that surgeon can't remove a pin in his left hand and—oh, you can't?

Hi, I saw online that Dr. ___ is a hand specialist. My son has a pin in his hand from a recent surgery done in Fargo. He needs to have it removed—oh—no one there will do it?

Hi, Dr. ___, this is Tracy Youngblom again. You did surgery on my son in March and put a pin in his left hand. We are wondering if you must remove it; we can't find anyone else who will do it. Please call me back so we can schedule that.

Hi—why not?

Hi—we have insurance.

Hi. (*Pause*). He will? When can we schedule that appointment? Tomorrow? Thank you so much.

Scene 2

In Dr.'s office. Mother, Elias, and Dr. ___ sit in an exam room.

DR. ___:

Well, young man, you've had quite an ordeal. Tell me how it's been.

Elias and Doctor bend toward each other, exchange words that are heard only as murmurs.

ELIAS:

How are you going to remove the pin? Will it hurt?

MOTHER/NARRATOR:

His dad joked that he could just take a big pliers and yank it out.

DR. ___:

Laughs. Opens a sterile bag; withdraws pliers from it. As he speaks, he slowly draws the pin out of Elias's left hand.

I may be able to get your U of M eye appointment moved up. It's been a pleasure to meet you, young man.

Scene 3

Courage Center, with Mother/Narrator, Therapists, Visitors, and Hospital Staff—props as needed.

As Therapist speaks, Elias does as she says.

THERAPIST:

Hey, we're going to try walking today between these parallel bars. It may hurt your foot a little, but we'll stretch first. You've got to get up and get moving.

Feel the bars? Okay, forward, one step at a time. Now backward. Now forward. Now backward. Now forward. Do you want to try turning around? Good, now walk forward to the end.

Excellent.

THERAPIST:

Today, we'll just walk in your room.

ELIAS (*Stands*):

I'm game. I want to get in that pool.

THERAPIST:

See if you can walk to the chair and back. I'll hold your arm.

Good job. Can you do it again?

ELIAS:

That's exhausting. But it feels good.

THERAPIST:

You are going to start using the walker; let's go out into the hallway.

That's great. That was about 150 feet.

We must get you walking farther so when you get home you don't have to use the wheelchair at all.

ELIAS:
That would be hard. There are stairs.

THERAPIST (*To Mother/Narrator, time passes between interactions*):
Are there rugs? You should move them—tripping hazard.

THERAPIST (*To Elias*):
Let's walk to the gym and back today.

It's time you start feeding yourself. And you can wheel yourself to the bathroom from now on—you don't need anyone to take you.

HOSPITAL STAFF:
Elias is way ahead of schedule. Two weeks ago, we thought he'd need to stay at least eight weeks, but we've decided on a tentative discharge date: June 5. That's a stay of only four weeks.

MOTHER/NARRATOR:
That's just over a week from now!

THERAPIST:
From now on, you need to call for your meds when it's time rather than rely on us to bring them to you.

MOTHER/NARRATOR (*To audience*):
When I stop and consider that it's only been ten weeks since the accident, I am amazed. Even though time has sometimes passed painfully slowly, the overall pace has been remarkably quick.

Elias is working hard on being independent. To observe him doing routine, daily things without sight touches me. He can't wait to get home.

Scene 4

Doctor's office waiting area. Elias in wheelchair, with Mother/ Narrator, Dad, and Hospital Staff.

NURSE:

Can you just fill out this paperwork? (*Holds papers out toward Elias.*)

DAD (*Taking papers*):

Let's see, I think I know your name and date of birth.

ELIAS:

Why do I have to have an eye exam? I can't see anything.

MOTHER/NARRATOR:

It's required to confirm your condition—before we go to that specialist at the U of M.

DAD:

Any history of stomach disorders?

ELIAS:

Yeah, I'm hungry all the time.

In an exam room.

ELIAS:

I see flashes of light sometimes. Does that mean I'll be able to see again?

Doctor performs eye exam. He exits then returns, holding a paper, hands it to Dad.

MOTHER/NARRATOR (*To audience*):

Here's what the doctor wrote in the letter we took home for verification: *Traumatic Optic Atrophy from MVA.* We had seen that abbreviation before: *MVA.* We finally figured it out: *Motor Vehicle Accident.* Such clinical terms to describe our stark reality.

Different doctor's office—the eye specialist at the U of M. Elias, Dad, Mother/Narrator, Doctor sit in chairs in an exam room.

MOTHER/NARRATOR:

If there's something that can be done, we want to start doing it.

Doctor (*Shuffling papers*):

It looks like his blindness was caused by one of several factors. I don't think there's any way to know for sure.

DAD:
We want to know if there's any chance of his seeing again.

DOCTOR:
Aren't you here because of a malpractice suit?

Dad and Mother/Narrator look surprised.

DOCTOR:
So you're not suing the surgeon?

DAD AND MOTHER/NARRATOR:
No!

DOCTOR:
His blindness is due to deadening of the optic nerves.

MOTHER/NARRATOR:
We know that. We've been reading about stem-cell therapy.

DAD:
We know there are some eye institutes doing research.

DOCTOR:
Stem-cell therapy isn't going to work. The optic nerves are more like the spinal cord; they branch out.

The most likely help will be Google-type glasses, where a video camera films what's in front of the person and sends those images to the brain via electrodes.

But be careful; people get excited about so-called miracle cures. Don't be tempted.

MOTHER/NARRATOR AND DAD (*Soberly*):
So he'll never see again?

ELIAS (*To all of us*):
The most important thing is that I'm alive.

Scene 5

Elias and Mother/Narrator in the car, a few days after the meeting with the eye specialist.

MOTHER/NARRATOR:

Do you want to stop home and see Maisie as long as we're out and about?

They walk slowly into the house, Elias holding Mother/Narrator's arm. He bumps into something, startles. Then he sits down in a chair.

ELIAS:

I can't believe I just ran into the kitchen counter in my own house.

Maisie enters, circles his feet. He reaches down to pet her, crying, head bowed. Mother/Narrator places her arm around Elias's shoulder.

MOTHER/NARRATOR (*Moves to face the audience*):

Home should be familiar and comforting; instead, it's a strange and foreign place.

My earliest and deepest grief, once we learned about Elias's blindness, erupted when I tried to imagine my son—my new son. He would never come in through the front door in the same way again, or throw his keys on the counter, or sit down, or tell me about his day. He would never take the stairs two at a time, or rush from job to job, or grab the sandwich I was handing him on his way out the door.

This reality is harsh; it is unfair. But maybe we are freest to grieve in the places where we are most comfortable.

She looks over her shoulder at Elias and Maisie.

This grief may season the honest struggle of coming to terms with the enormity of this new experience. It will still be a triumph to arrive home less than three months after the accident. Just because there is a sobering side does not negate that joy.

Once, the prospect of living at home and working on skills as an outpatient seemed as far away as the edge of the horizon in the desert—you can see it, but you can't walk there in a day. Once, the vision of a life free from nurses and aides and vital signs seemed to be a mirage. Now that reality is on us.

On that horizon are a confusion of appointments—eleven in the first three weeks! It marks the edge of the first stage. Another horizon awaits us, one we can't see yet. Going home is not an end, but a beginning, a continuation of the journey and the start of a new phase.

Truly, there will be struggles. Every day I wake with heaviness, thinking, *I don't want my son to be blind.*

I may not be ready. But the future—I mean, of course, Elias's future—doesn't wait on my readiness or acceptance.

WEIGHT

While Elias spent his twenty-two days in the ICU (I know because I counted), I lived in a nice, clean Days Inn near the hospital, where I quickly adjusted to life on the fly. I made do with four changes of clothes (some I had initially packed, some that Tim had brought from home during the first weekend after the accident) by visiting the laundromat once a week, a short walk across a parking lot from the hotel. There, I read from a book of David Sedaris essays (a gift from a friend) or sat with my chin in my hand, waiting for my clothes to dry, trying not to stare at the locals or attract the attention of families with children who were used to the routine. Their kids raced each other in wheeled carts or fed quarters into vending machines to purchase snacks that looked outdated. I sat tense and immobile and impatient, but still wondering if the Funyuns the boy next to me was munching were expired.

My diet was simple during that time. I ate my "free" breakfast at the hotel—Raisin Bran, or hard-boiled eggs and toast, or sometimes an orange. Then I ate lunch at the hospital cafeteria, usually salad from the bounteous salad bar. In the evening, I snacked on fruit or cheese and crackers in my hotel room. People had left me so much food! The amazing truth revealed itself: my normal life had contained a lot of excess (which is a nice way of saying I had been eating too much before). Here, in this intensely emotional time, much less than usual turned out to be enough. One night, a group of us went out to Kroll's Diner for dinner—celebrating some milestone—and I ate a whole patty melt and fries. I thought I would never be hungry again.

In the entire three weeks I lived at the hotel, I didn't go to the gym or consider exercising even once, though I had been a disciplined runner and a volleyball player for at least twenty years. In addition to my diet changing, my definition of exercising had changed: taking the stairs at the hotel or the hospital counted, as did walking the four blocks to the nearest mailbox several times a week to keep current with bills and thank-you cards. I had changed, too; circumstances bore down, rearranged my priorities, forced me to adjust my identity.

By early April, a couple of weeks into Elias's hospital stay, spring began to assert itself. Temperatures gradually warmed and the snow was melting. The world was splash and sluice, messy. I could identify. I didn't feel so stable myself—I felt, in fact, a little slushy.

My life during this time became markedly low key, everything pared down to essentials. But far from seeming difficult, my adjustments felt natural, organic, as if I were returning to a purer life. Even in less-than-ideal conditions, I put down roots and survived, with little fuss. I lost some weight as a result—my jeans were looser, I could snug up the belt an extra notch—though precisely how many pounds will remain a mystery as I never go near a scale if I can help it.

When Elias moved to Regency Hospital and then Courage Center, I was able to return to my previous routines, to go home at night and sleep in my own bed. People brought us meals, or I left Regency at night to grab some food at Byerly's, so I ate dinner again, swallowing routinely, somewhat unwillingly. Eventually, I began to cook again. Undoubtedly, I gained back some of the weight I'd lost.

Yet I am surprised, now that Elias has returned home. I still feel the same and my clothes still fit the same, but my body feels heavier than ever because I have ingested, besides more food, heaps of grief I never thought I could stomach. Resuming my three-mile runs is difficult; I am out of shape and awkward, and flashes of bedside sweat and worry rerun in my head like scenes from a bad horror film. Getting out of bed each morning requires concentration and effort, a will to haul my ponderous mass of affliction with me as I move through my day.

If the weight of emotional reality were literal, if grief were efficacious, I would weigh, by now, six hundred pounds. My physical body, alas, doesn't show it. *Little bastard*. Such a betrayal.

I carry my excess carefully, uneasily, aware that it is invisible weight. My shoes don't make the tiled floors of grocery stores creak or bow; struts don't groan when I sit in my car. Still, when speaking with strangers—cashiers or casual acquaintances—I want to unload some of my weight into words. To their innocuous greetings—*How are you today? Did you find everything you need?*—I want to blurt out:

My son was recently blinded by a drunk driver who blew a .198 at two o'clock in the afternoon and was driving the wrong way down the interstate. But you have a good day, too.

That, of course, I won't do. I will keep swallowing, keep bearing this heaviness privately, rather than revealing how large I've become and why.

EAT IT ALL

When my three boys were growing up, Elias often didn't finish his dinner. He was a picky eater at best, a dawdler. He would sit at the table for a half hour after everyone else had finished, pushing food around on his plate with his fork. According to the rules of the day, not finishing dinner meant he got no bedtime snack. He knew that and accepted it, refusing to ask for pity or an exception. Once, after he hadn't eaten, our family went out to some gathering where they were serving cake. I overheard him tell the host, *I can't have any because I didn't eat my supper.*

I remember one night when he was four or five. He had refused dinner as usual, but I heard him crying upstairs in his bed. I was trying to study downstairs for a graduate class, my head bent over an anthology of modernist poets. His muffled sobs broke my concentration—and my heart. I knew all about hunger, about pain so sharp it makes you cry. I was adjusting—we were all adjusting—to Rich's and my divorce. Devouring my course readings helped me dull the pain of the lost marriage. Though Elias had never asked me for food, his crying was persuasive that night; it convinced me. To appease us both, I trudged upstairs with his favorite yogurt and a spoon and sat with him while he ate.

He never let me forget it. For years afterward, as he continued to skip dinner and then discover that he was famished, he'd plead, *Remember that time you brought me a yogurt?*

Tonight for dinner I have made something good, something Elias will like—comfort food: chicken with pan sauce, mashed potatoes, steamed green beans. He feels his way to the kitchen table, sits down firmly in the chair formerly assigned to me. I have ceded my place at the end of the table because it's the easiest spot for him to get to.

He has been home from the hospital for less than a week. It is hard work for him to find his way to the bathroom and to meals, hard work to avoid tripping over the dog. She is sweet but not brilliant, though she seems to sense that something is different. She lay down fully on his chest the other night, snuggling in when he decided to watch TV downstairs. (*Listen to TV, you mean*, I want to correct him, but I bite my tongue.) This is something she's never done, but surely she can't understand the fullness of what he's going through—can she?

He must move slowly through the familiar territory of the house, intensely concentrating. His large bedroom, once a benefit, once the envy of his brothers, is now a liability. He has gotten lost in it—a brief embarrassing panic, he confesses reluctantly.

I don't know what to say in the face of these layers of impossibility. In this first week, I have often stood silently, watching him navigate stairs he once would have bounded up or down, two at a time. Tonight, too, instead of providing words, I have cooked something good, attempting to make him happy about food at least. Maybe that simple happiness will be contagious, spread out and affect his mood about other things. I believe I am trying to help him adjust, but on some level I know I am also trying to make myself feel better.

During dinner, I talk, keeping up a steady stream of chatter about the upcoming week—hand therapy, jaw therapy, physical therapy—the many appointments we have on our list. In my recital of the week's work, I am trying to boost him over the wall of his own discouragement, transfer to him inner strength I believe he needs, but even as I prattle on, I hear my own voice: chirruping, hollow.

He sits in his adopted chair, not eating, not even tasting this food he used to crave. Instead, he hangs his head, and his hands curl in loose fists on either side of his plate, framing the meal. His tears fall onto his dinner, into his lap. I get up then, put my arm around his shoulders, and keep quiet—finally.

I can't tell him it's going to be okay. The claim is not only a cliché but it may also not be true. As I embrace him, he unclenches himself, not looking at me—but why would he look at me?—pushes his chair back loudly, exits the kitchen, and feels his way to his room, a grand gesture, executed with exacting slowness.

The rest of us (Tim and I, Elias's girlfriend) remain at the table, the scrape of his chair legs still echoing through the room. We fuss over our dinner, take small bites, feign contentment. *This is so good*, we lie.

When he comes down again later, after the table has been cleared and wiped, dishes loaded into the dishwasher, I don't offer him leftovers. Instead, I suggest ice cream. We all drive to Two Scoops in Anoka, order our cones, sit on slatted wooden benches outside, and enjoy the beautiful June night. We lick our ice cream and our fingers with unimpeded delight.

I have never suggested dessert in place of dinner before. My former self would have rebelled against it. But I am not sure I would recognize my former self, and anyway there are no rules now; perhaps there never should have been rigid rules in the first place. We all have to fight our way through this adjustment, making up rules as we go.

KEY FOB

A fancy key fob came with my newly acquired, slightly used car. It is still an odd sensation to have a car with such an accessory, though I've now owned it for a couple of years. When I press the fob's various buttons, I enter a kingdom: my own private domain. When I hold it in my hand, I maintain control. I reach into my purse where it rests, snug inside a pocket, to reassure myself it is still there.

I am constantly amazed at how this car acquiesces to my will. From across a parking lot, I press one button and the car chirps to life and unlocks. Is this not the ultimate power? What should I make of the tyranny of the fob, its easily conferred authority?

More than once in years past, when forced into an intractable position, I'd bought a trimmed-down version of an already cheap vehicle: a hatchback Hyundai Accent, a Toyota Yaris, an old but reliable Subaru station wagon. They'd had crank windows, push-button locks, no cruise control, no air conditioning—certainly, no fancy key fobs.

But this new car is a Honda Accord, bought to replace the beloved Accord that Nate had totaled in 2005, right after getting his driver's license, when, burning to show off to his friends, he had taken a corner too fast, lost control, and driven into a yard, almost ramming the front end into an elderly couple's house. He'd run into a large bush instead, which had prevented disaster. Luckily, neither he nor the friends he'd decided to drive home from school before his work shift had gotten hurt, but it had been hard for me to be grateful for that fact because I had only given him permission to drive my car to school and work on that one day.

The totaling of the original Accord was a loss. That car had represented a giant step toward independence for me. I had bought it when it was only three years old—I, a single parent, who didn't feel grown up or even confident most of the time. Buying it and driving it made me feel less like an imposter.

I'd settled for a Hyundai Accent after Nate totaled the Accord because it was all I could afford with the insurance money, and I couldn't manage a car payment. But, in all the years since, I'd longed for another Accord.

Acquiring the new Accord coincided with another new accord I made with myself: no more skimping. *You can afford power doors and windows—you deserve them.* No more tuna cans on wheels—that was what Caleb and Nate had dubbed the Accent.

Before Tim and I bought the new car, in 2013, I'd watched its price for several months on the dealer's website. I wanted the car, but I also wanted a good deal. Eventually, the price dropped—no one seemed to want the manual transmission—so I pulled the trigger and bought it. It felt luxurious—a new sensation, a welcome one—to drive around in it, with its sleek silver flanks, its gray upholstery, its moon roof. It was the first car I'd ever driven—except for the cheaply made Accent—that had been manufactured in the same decade in which I'd bought it.

A second accord I made with myself was that my children would never drive this car. By 2013, none of them lived at home anymore, and I thought the days of sharing vehicles were surely over. In years past, when Caleb had taken the Accent to work, Elias had taken the Civic to his drumline rehearsal. Or if Nate had used the Hyundai, Caleb had driven the old Subaru. Often I was left at home with no car at all. But I rarely did anything alone in those days.

Things were different now, I reasoned; all three boys were mostly grown. To make that reality visible, I decreed, *This car is mine. I am its sole driver.* I felt fully justified in my decision.

Then, in March 2015, Tim and I spent my spring break in Napa, California, visiting his daughter. Elias drove us to the airport in my Accord. At the time, he was in possession of the 2002 Civic I'd bequeathed to him, but it was in no shape to haul three people and luggage to the airport, strewn as it was with fast-food wrappers, drumsticks, CDs, and notebooks. So, the Accord was the better option.

All week while we were relaxing, tasting wine, and enjoying fine weather, I wondered whether he was driving my car to work and back. In my mind, that would have qualified as *sneaking around.*

I spoke to Elias briefly on the Saturday night we returned home. By then he was in Fargo, visiting friends, and my sister Terri had picked us up from the airport. Though I asked him about Maisie and the time of his return on Monday, I refrained from asking about my car. I had peeked into the backseat as we were unloading our suitcases and discovered remnants of a meal he had taken to work after dropping us off a week ago—a pint glass jar caked with his favorite go-to breakfast, overnight oats. I would leave that for him to deal with later. I had no idea if he'd driven my car at any other time during the week, but I put my questions on hold until I could talk to him in person.

But on Monday, his drive home from Fargo was interrupted. His life was interrupted. My worries about the car became ridiculous to me then—petty, as they had always been . . . as perhaps I had always been.

I have since altered my accord. My children can now drive my car—those who can still drive. In fact, I insist on it, and I seek out opportunities to make the Accord available. *Please, Nate, take my car to Belle Plaine to visit your grandparents.* However, I made that change too late.

I don't know why I didn't suggest that Elias take the Accord to Fargo that weekend. I could've driven the Civic to school on Monday—for one day. The fact that I am wondering about it now suggests that I'd considered it then, too, but decided to stick to my steadfast agreement with myself.

The Accord is a bigger, newer car, boasting front and side airbags. The Civic, though a reliable vehicle, had limitations. For instance, it had only a front airbag in the steering column. That airbag did deploy in the accident, but the impact had come primarily from the unprotected driver's side. Moreover, the drunk driver was in a Lincoln Town Car, a much heavier vehicle than the Civic.

I wonder now: could the Accord, with its dual airbags, have softened the impact, protected Elias, and preserved his eyesight?

I fear it could have.

I spin along in the groove my life is making, my own private orbit, sluggish and remote and alone with this guilt.

THE OLD FAMILIAR

He was seventeen, tall and upright and angry, all sinew and fury. Whatever he said was meant to infuriate me, especially this announcement: *It's your fault I'm not doing my homework!*

I stared at him, speechless. Or perhaps I stammered out a shocked question: *How can that be?*

He responded, *You keep asking me if I've done it. You're putting too much pressure on me.*

We stood feet apart, though in all ways that counted we were miles apart. He was failing junior English, refusing to do his homework despite my pleas and threats. *If you don't get your grades up, you'll have to quit marching band*, I'd said, because marching band was consuming all of his free time, both after school and on weekends. On show Saturdays, he was away from home for fourteen or fifteen hours at a stretch.

In my mind, my threat was a way to create a logical consequence. Isn't that how parents are supposed to respond—by setting boundaries and sticking to them? However, my ultimatum enraged him. He doubled down, dug in his heels, became, if possible, even more stubbornly committed to opposing me than he'd been before.

Years earlier, on a fine summer day when Elias was about ten, I was feeling generous, proud of myself and my children. So I drove alone to Dairy Queen to buy all three boys Blizzards, an extravagant gesture that I could barely afford. Elias had asked for a medium, the same size that his older brothers had requested. But I got him a small because he was still little and he was picky, with a sporadic appetite even on his best days.

At home I distributed the treats, happy to think my children would be pleased with me. But on Elias's face was a look of pure disgust. Turning his gaze from the cup in his hand to me, he launched into a tirade: *I told you to get me a medium. You got me a small. You're treating me like a baby. You don't think I can eat as much as Caleb and Nate. But I can. I'm not a baby. I wanted a medium. You got me a small. I'm not a baby, but you're treating me like a baby.*

Then he cocked his arm and heaved his small Blizzard across the wide expanse of the kitchen. The cup thudded into a corner cupboard and splattered, rivulets of thick ice cream sliding down onto the floor.

My mouth opened, a circle of indignant surprise. *Go to your room*, I pointed.

As Elias stomped up the stairs, I immediately realized my mistake. Hurrying after him, I yelled through his closed door, *Get downstairs and clean up*, pointing again, even though he couldn't see my gesture.

He erupted from the room and raged past me, back down the stairs. He strode across the kitchen and grabbed a dishrag. Still steaming, I leaned against the doorframe to watch, arms folded. I maintained this stance for a while, observing. I tried to figure out what had made him so angry. He'd wasted food and money and made a mess—but for what? To prove a point?—that I had offended him?

As I watched, Elias scooped up blobs of ice cream and dumped them into the DQ cup. When the cup was full, he emptied it into the sink. Then, wetting the dishrag, he rubbed down the cupboard door. Rinsing and wetting it again and again, he cleaned the door thoroughly, even inserting a single finger into an edge of the cloth to wipe out the crevices and paying special attention to the corners.

Against my will, my arms began to relax. I watched as he crouched, not complaining now but seriously devoted to this job, oblivious of my presence. Soon, I was smiling. Eventually, I went into the living room so he wouldn't see how proud of him I was.

Today is Tuesday. Elias has insisted on going to this marching band rehearsal, even though he just got home from the hospital last Friday. So now I am pulling into the Blaine High School parking lot.

We'd spent the past weekend in Fargo at his behest: attending a wedding, visiting the ICU staff at Sanford Medical Center, connecting with the surgeon who'd repaired his facial fractures (the same surgeon who'd cried when we found out about Elias's blindness). I witnessed this doctor embracing my son (whom before he had only seen confined to a bed) in the hospital hallway, all of their eyes—seeing and unseeing—wet with tears.

In the school parking lot, I unload the wheelchair from the trunk, unfold it, ease Elias into it, wheel him toward the cluster of people who swarm toward him. A crowd of band-booster moms forms a line to hug him. Students, for the most part, hang back, shyly amazed.

Within a few weeks, the booster moms will present him with a gift: a staff jacket they've ordered and paid for, with Elias's name embroidered on the front in letters and in Braille.

On parent-teacher conference day, Elias and I sat across the table from his English teacher. We were discussing his report card.

He's going to have to take summer school, the teacher said. *There's no way he can pass junior English now.*

I was trying to keep calm, not erupt. But a teacher's son—my son—in summer school? I couldn't accept it.

I have been trying to get him to do his homework all year, I stammered, incensed. *Now it's too late. I guess he's going to have to quit marching band after all.*

The teacher, a stranger to me until that day, sat up straight, with a sudden, serious expression on her face. *Oh, no, not that,* she said. *That would be bad. Don't take away something he loves.*

Hiding my shock—who was she to dictate my decisions as a parent?—I asserted, *But there must be some consequence. He's basically refused to do his homework.*

She smiled at me, trying to be kind. *It won't be worth it,* she said. *I was that kid. The only reason I stayed in school was music. If he doesn't have that, what reason will he have left to try?*

Elias has been home from the hospital now for a couple of weeks. We have been active. Today I drive him to Waconia, Minnesota, for a parade, an hour from our home. I offer to push him in his wheelchair along the parade route, just behind the band.

But first the drum section that he directs must warm up. I wheel him over to where they have gathered, and he stands up. I back his wheelchair out of the way, pretend it does not exist (that I do not exist).

Okay, let's run through the opening, he says to the semicircle of students, who are unaware of the effort it costs him to stand on his own, who may or may not realize—or fully fathom—that he can't see them.

The students play the drum part that he had written for them. *That was pretty good, but I think you can make it better,* he says.

Let's go around the circle. Each of you, tell me one small thing you can correct in the next run-through.

They go around, these awkward high school students, shy but happy to do what he has asked.

Now that you've said it, just do it, he says.

He raises his hands and begins conducting again.

WRESTLING WITH
THE STORY

When Elias lay in his bed at Regency Hospital, resting in the evenings or between therapy sessions, adjusting to the darkness that was now his sight, I cast around for ways to entertain him. I told jokes; I babbled, describing the weather or my latest teaching adventure.

Darkness tired him. Conversation wore him out. To help him keep alert, I handed him a carved wooden bird that someone had made for him to encourage tactile stimulation. Or I gave him a foam purple dinosaur that another person had given him to squeeze for strength. I accepted my role: to minimize Elias's down time. (It's so easy to let the world slip away when you can't see its bright contrasts.) My pelvis rested against his bedrail, as if I could thrust him into a new life, as I had at his birth.

All of his regular family visitors tried to interest him in various tactile activities. And then, finally, we thought about books. Books—yes! Reading, yes! What a way to reenter the world! Elias had been given some books that weren't capturing his interest, but I pursued this course with energy. We would revive him by reading to him. Doesn't everyone love a story?

I didn't consult him but instead went home and chose a young-adult novel, *The Tale of Despereaux*, by Kate DiCamillo. I don't know why I chose it, but it stood out to me as I perused my shelves. I hadn't read it for a long time, not since I had taught it in a children's literature class years ago, but I did remember loving it.

From the first page, he was hooked; he was sniffing along the trail of the story. All of our family shared in the triumph and took turns reading: me, Rich, my sister Trish, my mom. As we read, we fell deeper into our mission: we needed to give Elias something to look forward to.

Amazingly, as we read, we began to look forward, too. DiCamillo's story moved, gestured, beckoned us all toward some idea of a future. We kept our noses to the scent of its narrative. The experience of living in this world moved us: we loved cheering for another person's, another character's, future. The book mimicked our general quest—to usher Elias into a worthwhile life—something we may not have been thinking of consciously, much less speaking of aloud.

The true power of stories is that their unspooling seems inevitable—a match lit, a wick that must burn. Following that trail provides a future and a hope, a substitute for the stories of real life, which often end badly, as we so clearly knew.

Recently, I read a passage in Michael Pollan's engaging book, *The Omnivore's Dilemma*:

> *I'd violated the Chekhovian dramatic rule: Having intro-duced a loaded gun in Act One, the curtain can't come down until it is fired. I might miss, but the gun had to be fired. That at least seemed to be the narrative imperative.*[1]

This passage helped me realize that, while reading *Despereaux* to my blind son, we had all responded to that "narrative imperative," our sense of what moves a story along. One action directly leads to another *because it must*. In a good story, all elements have to be accounted for. Details in fiction are not the same as props in a play, but they are still essential. I can supply terms from many English literature classes: backstory, foreshadowing.

But Elias's accident had made no sense. Part of the nonsense was that we kept referring to the accident as *his*, as if it were his responsibility. There had been no loaded gun, no sign or portent. In that sense, it was not a story at all, though I was tasked to keep telling it.

Nor could I predict any long-term outcome. While he dozed at Regency, I watched him for signs of what might come next: there was nothing that I could predict. The simple act of reading *The Tale of Despereaux* gave us all a sense of progress, of normalcy, of hope.

Though most stories subscribe to this idea, there are examples in literature of stories that refuse to offer the expected. Eventually, as I struggled to adjust, I was reminded of a few of these famous variations on the principle.

The first that came to mind was Thomas Hardy's poem about the sinking of the *Titanic*, "The Convergence of the Twain." As I reread it, I realized that, whether or not anything could have predicted the disaster, Hardy chose to solve its mystery by declaring that it had had a divine purpose: an "Immanent Will" had brought down the "Pride of Life" and "vaingloriousness"—not of the ship itself, but of the ship's creation, its prideful conception. Hardy made meaning by reinforcing a familiar moral: *Pride goes before a fall*. The fancy ship at the bottom of the sea said it all:

Over mirrors meant
To glass the opulent
The sea-worm crawls—grotesque, slimed, dumb, indifferent.[2]

In Hardy's vision, fate determined everything—that "Spinner of Years"—and though lives were lost, the ship—and the people?—got what they ultimately deserved. Most likely, Hardy was using *God* as a synonym for *fate*, a sentiment I saw echoed in many comments on the CaringBridge site, especially in the early days of Elias's recovery.

I couldn't apply Hardy's wisdom to our situation. Doing so would mean accepting that God had caused Elias's accident in order to do something, to make some point—but what? Teach him a lesson? Make Elias's path in the world clear? Bring down his pride? Those answers enraged me, as did some of the early comments on the CaringBridge site that seemed to point to this cruel conclusion.

I was also reminded of Robert Frost's poem "Out, Out—" which tells a strange and tragic story, one with no conflict, no foreshadowing, no cause and effect. Yet the speaker attempts to justify the poem's main event by imposing rationality on the unforeseen, the accidental. This example felt much closer to home.

The poem illuminates a tragedy, an actual death. The speaker goes so far as to assign agency to the saw that takes the young boy's arm and life:

> At the word, the saw,
> As if to prove saws knew what supper meant,
> Leaped out at the boy's hand, or seemed to leap—
> He must have given the hand.[3]

Frost's speaker tries to make a rational story out of disparate elements, but there can be no satisfying justification for such random and fatal violence. The boy has not, as the speaker suggests, "given the hand." But perhaps that is another rendition of the impulse to make up a reason if one doesn't seem automatically clear. We do want explanations, largely in order to tell ourselves and the world that life is not, after all, completely random.

Most notable in the poem is the characterization of the saw, the real villain. In the first several lines, the speaker notes twice that the saw "snarled and rattled"; these lines make the saw out to be the aggressor. However, anyone who works around power tools—I did as a child at my grandparents' farm—knows one has to respect the power, handle it with caution, but not refuse to handle it. That's how one lives alongside it and prevents accidents.

I could not accept the fatalism this poem offered either. The poem's subject was more personal than Hardy's subject. This poem suggested that Elias was to blame: wasn't he the boy and the hand? wasn't the other driver the saw? Yet he'd had nothing to do with his accident—except that *his* was the one car that couldn't swerve completely out of the way. But he had tried, I reminded myself; the two cars' fronts had barely kissed. Only about a foot of each one had collided—the two drivers' side headlights—and Elias's car, careening away at an angle, had become subject to the physics of that motion and had spun and skidded and rolled far out of the way.

There was a nurse at Regency Hospital who, on the first night she spent caring for my son, derailed our composure. I was standing to the side as I often did, leaning on a heat vent near the window, trying to blend in. I never wanted to draw attention to myself. I wanted hospital staff to notice my son, how unusual he was—a star survivor, a wounded young man whose politeness never failed. Even when in pain he said please and thank you to hospital staff.

This nurse, when she entered the room, silently took Elias's good right hand in both of hers, sandwiching it. Then, without introducing herself, she pronounced, *God has spared you.*

She continued, orating a ten-minute monologue about how God was going to use him hereafter, how important it was for him not to give up. I stayed to the side, silenced by the powerful timbre of her voice. She had read his chart, clearly. I trusted her for that.

But silence can be acquiescence. I couldn't see any evidence of a divine will in the accident and the ensuing blindness, though I didn't say anything that night.

I wish now I had stood up—for myself, for Elias—and had told that nurse how much I hated all this pressure to justify a senseless tragedy. I didn't share her vision or her faith that there was a plan. I hated that there was no conflict—no visible one—and no impending crisis, just a young man driving home on a familiar route toward a future so bright you couldn't even stare directly at it.

I hate most of all, especially now, that I have to keep repeating this not-story, our story, my story: *Suddenly, out of nowhere, disaster struck.* What hope can this story offer?

The accident was a portal that forced us into a new life. But this is no Narnia. We are not going to set a dark world on fire. Even now—when the prospects are good—the other side is not a welcoming place.

So I chew my rations of bitterness and peer ahead, squinting.

PART II

IMPACT

I've been using the word *impact* a lot during these past weeks, now that I've returned to the classroom for the fall semester of 2015. My job is unlikely to be interrupted by something so personal again. It's research paper time, when students choose and narrow topics, consider how to take a position, to divine what they really think. Often I suggest considering implications, the impact of one thing on another—fast food on childhood obesity, for instance, or standardized testing on classroom practices.

When I was a college student, I didn't have a good sense of the word. That's why, after having had two wisdom teeth extracted one fall afternoon when I was an undergraduate, I headed to the next day's 8 a.m. theology class, impervious to any impact the surgery might have on me.

After several minutes I apparently put my head down on my desk, then stood up suddenly in the aisle and fainted dead away, falling forward between two rows of desks. I didn't hit anything on the way down, other than the floor that rose up to meet me. But one learns one's vocabulary and remembers it according to experience. The next year, when I had my final two wisdom teeth out, I had the word and its meaning at my disposal. I was more cautious.

Impact, of course, means a lot of things: strong influence, forceful consequence, the violent interaction of troops in combat, the striking of one body against another.

Cars have bodies. We call fixing them after collisions *body work*. We go to body shops, and sometimes I have seen my sons run a palm against the fender of a newly waxed car as tenderly as if it were a woman's hip.

In the case of my son Elias, the bodies of the cars crashed into each other, resulting in a high-speed impact. Each vehicle was going about seventy miles per hour, give or take (though the driver who hit my son was drunk, going the wrong way down the interstate, one senseless action impacting another). Witnesses said there was an explosion.

The literal part of my brain is curious, hungry for precision: explosion as in sound? or debris? or both? The answer must be both: powder from the air bags hung in the air for several minutes afterward, I was told. Both drivers' physical bodies also suffered from the force of the impact, and they were the only bodies to survive. Both cars were totaled.

I find it impossible to visualize this impact, though I can record its basic details: blur of action, booming sound, bodies of the cars twisting and torquing, my son's body inside the car, thrown backward, forward, bones cracking and breaking through the skin, insides bruised and sliced by the force of the seatbelt, facial bones shifting, the beautiful symmetry of his face askew. But even that image hasn't stayed with me, nor can I imagine the unretouched version, the version that the paramedics found when they approached the car: everywhere there must have been blood, glass, terror, disorientation.

I don't want to imagine it. Even without a clear picture, I feel a certain impact in my own body these months later, a sudden constrained horror that takes my breath or forces it out as a punch to the gut would or stops me midstep to release a shudder. It is heavy, this impact—not painful but forceful. Unpredictable.

The body absorbs and the body reacts. Somehow, Elias's body absorbed the impact without brain injury, without spinal cord injury. He was badly hurt, but we have him still, his personality intact. The swelling, however, was a reaction that created a blockage, prevented blood flow to his optic nerve, and took away his sight.

In a few weeks, he will have an opportunity to read a victim impact statement in court, when the drunk driver hears her sentence. Will the statement be more like absorption or reaction? He has absorbed a lot in the past months: drugs and fluids, oxygen, painful realizations, the constant love and surveillance of family and friends, prayers. His reactions have been consistently, impressively upbeat; he has had rare moments of distress, hopelessness—rare and short-lived. In court he'll talk about the impact of the accident on his life and potential teaching career, but he won't use the word *victim*. His mind will not absorb that meaning; he reacts strongly against it. In a recent interview, he vowed that he wouldn't let *the stupid decision of one person control my life*. He refuses to grant her that power.

My hips ache more and more these days during sleep, my body's reaction to aging. The pain itself is not new, just a copy of the pain I experienced during pregnancy. Waiting for each boy to enter the world, my hip joints expanded, creaked, groaned; a haunting discomfort left me sleepless for many nights. I may be absorbing the ache of my child again, not the ache of his body growing, but of his mind and spirit—the fighting and resisting and twisting of my own reactions, a sympathetic growth.

TOTAL WRECK

By early November 2015, we had survived for eight months post-accident—two-thirds of a year. How was time supposed to affect me? Part of me thought, *Eight months—that's a long time!* Another part of me felt sluggish and contemplative.

It's been eight months. Can I wake up now?

Rich, Elias, and I made our way to the Minnesota state patrol headquarters in Detroit Lakes to visit the remains of the car that had been totaled in the accident. It was strange to visit an object, but the idea had been Elias's, so we were going to do it. We followed his lead when he could see a way forward. His pre-trip instructions to Rich and me had been clear: *When we get there, you two should go somewhere else. I want to be by myself when I first see it.*

We had gotten used to Elias's use of the word *see* in normal conversation; it no longer sounded odd. However, as it turned out, Elias didn't get his wish. The state trooper in charge met us as we drove up to the entrance gate—the same trooper who'd repeatedly searched the accident scene for Elias's lost wallet.

We parked and got out, then followed this trooper into a field covered in rows upon rows of wrecks, a graveyard for totaled cars that had been impounded pending the conclusion of investigations. Finally, after a vigorous hike, the trooper stopped at our vehicle: the silver Civic that Elias had driven back and forth to Fargo countless times.

The car was nearly unrecognizable: its spider-webbed, splintered windshield was laid like a textured bedspread over the hood. The driver's door was gone, and so was the entire roof. (*Where is it?* I wondered, swishing through tall weeds behind the car.) The frame along the base of the driver's door was exposed: accordioned, curved into a ragged inward arc. The dash had been forced forward (backward?) until it was almost touching the front seats. The driver's bucket seat was torqued sideways and to the left, the seatbelt severed as if with scissors, frayed ends dangling. At the bottom lip of the driver's door, heavy steel bars, like those used in the construction of tall buildings, snaked out at crazy angles. (*Rebar?* Some part of my brain supplied the word.) The airbag, a deflated balloon, hung from the steering column.

Inside the car was chaos: glass shards scattered like confetti, chunks of ripped plastic in the front seats and, in the backseat, a college student's collection of detritus: Tupperware, several of my good forks, Mountain Dew cans, fast-food bags, coins, sheet music, Chapstick, CDs.

We described what we could see to our son, who stood between us, upright and stock-still in the chilly breeze. After he had pictured the sight internally, he began to get his bearings, carefully touching the car, including the opening where the driver's door had once hung. Then, to my surprise, he pivoted suddenly and sat down in the driver's seat.

I didn't know what I had been expecting, but not this. I wanted to dissuade him, but he'd already taken action, and a pointed look from Rich kept me quiet.

Elias sat sideways in the seat, his legs angled outward. Because the dash had moved, he couldn't get them under the steering wheel (though at the time of the accident, they had been). His face dimmed and brightened as he leaned backward and to his right, his legs outside the car, to locate the shift knob, move it through the gears. We saw him smile at the familiar click when he shifted into reverse.

We moved closer and saw, now, something we couldn't have seen before. Jutting down from the steering column, where his right leg should have been, a heavy, wide, flat piece of metal had descended. About two inches across and a quarter of an inch thick, it would have sliced through his femur if his leg had been there. We mentioned it to him so he could feel for it.

I had the cruise on, he said, *so that leg was off to the side.*

He wondered aloud if we could find the key, which we had all forgotten about in the intervening months since the accident. Rich and I gingerly sifted through the mess of the interior, doubting the outcome. But there it was, in a pile of glass and debris on the front passenger's seat. We couldn't imagine how it had ended up there, but we didn't have to understand this mystery in order to accept it.

Would you like to see the other car? the trooper asked from somewhere close.

We were startled; we had forgotten he had led us here, was waiting for us.

The other driver's car squatted next to Elias's Civic. Its front end looked worse than the Civic's: it was compacted, pushed in, snub-nosed.

I did some damage to her vehicle, Elias said, feeling his way around the exterior.

He seemed proud of what his Civic had done to her Town Car; he was kind of excited about it. But he would never have wanted *her* to be damaged.

Recently we had seen her in court, our first glimpse of her. She'd been in a wheelchair: the accident had injured her ankle, the only injury she sustained, as far as we knew. To me, that outcome was the opposite of poetic justice. She had almost killed my son, yet she remained basically uninjured. When I saw her, a swell of anger threatened to overtake me; I almost rose from my chair. All through the proceeding, I avoided looking at her. I sat with my fists clenched in my lap or I clutched the wooden railing in front of me. Whenever I turned in her direction and inadvertently saw the back of her head, I thought I would choke, or faint, or vomit.

Elias had listened to her that day in court. *I don't remember what happened*, she had said. He responded in a way that made our family proud. After the hearing, as we stood in the court-house lobby, rather than giving into anger, he said, *She's worse off than me. I'm doing way better than she is.*

After looking at both cars on that November day, after thanking the trooper, leaving the headquarters, making our way back to Rich's Subaru, we spent the entirety of our three-hour-drive home discussing our momentous trip.

Elias admitted he had expected flashbacks, but there were none. His overwhelming impression—and ours—was that he shouldn't have survived the accident. The Civic was a total wreck.

Mixed emotions—nostalgia and triumph, fear and hope and gratitude—sat with us. We realized our lives had been given to us, repeatedly. How else could we respond except to make good use of them?

Back home, Elias put the Civic's key on a chain and wore it around his neck, to help him remember and to push him forward.

During the past eight months, he hadn't seemed to need much additional motivation to push forward with his life. Just a few weeks ago, he had dressed up for Halloween with his best friend, Jared. They had donned matching pirate suits. Elias had elected to wear two eye patches, a costume that said it all: *Here I am. Deal with it.*

GROOVES

When I kept vigil at the hospital in Fargo, my days were filled with chaotic emotions that battled for supremacy: worry, fear, anxiety, elation about my son's progress. To cope, I needed to pretend I was just going about my business, so I developed a routine at the hospital, along with a parallel routine at my hotel "home."

Though I set no alarm, I woke in time to eat breakfast at the hotel. After that, I snugged up my collar, exited the building, strode to my reliable Honda Accord, started it up. The engine always turned over immediately.

My route to the hospital never varied: 19th Avenue East to 10th Street North, then south to 12th Avenue and east to Broadway. I drove south for four blocks. I parked in the main lot.

The same CDs unspooled in my car's player for the duration of my stay: albums by the Civil Wars, the Milk Carton Kids, the Beatles. The familiar songs and lyrics pushed away thoughts of death or invited them in.

Day after day, when their CD played, I heard the Milk Carton Kids sing, "Freedom comes from being unafraid of the heartache that can plague a man."[4] I sang along, though I always fell silent as one particular line neared: "Hold the hand that leads you, there's no god here to believe."[5] I couldn't say those words; I was afraid that any lapse of faith invited by singing them would jinx Elias's steady recovery. Just before the words eased out of the speaker, I would fast-forward to the next song.

After parking, I climbed three flights of stairs, pushed a button on the wall outside of the ICU, and waited for the automatic doors to open, for their wide mouth to swallow me, to press me forward into the stomach of recovery: room 308, with its sounds—rhythmic beeps, the bangs of a cast on the bed's sideboard, the moans and groans—and sights—tubes, stiff limbs, swelling, awkwardness. I was like Jonah in the whale, though I didn't want to be expelled. My purpose was to endure. My only venture out of his room was to the hospital cafeteria, for lunch.

My evening routine was similarly circumscribed. Back at the hotel, I performed my essential duties: made phone calls and wrote emails to update friends and family members who hadn't physically been at the hospital; sent instructions and handouts to the colleagues who were teaching my classes. Then I munched on cheese and crackers, watched TV, and occasionally tried to read. I fell asleep by 10:30: a deep mindless sleep that led me into morning without fanfare. I feel a tinge of guilt when I admit that those three weeks included some of the best sleep I've ever had.

This groove became my life. I could not—did not want to—divert from the usual. I needed to follow the same track each day, a pattern that allowed me to forget the strangeness of the circumstances. As someone commented on an early CaringBridge post, *It's amazing how we can admit the unthinkable into our everyday reality.* I did not realize how committed I was to my routine until Tim suggested I might find a cheaper hotel. An automatic, visceral no erupted from my mouth, almost a shout.

More than a year later, I am still hyperaware of my continuing commitment to routine (and hyperaware that I am aware of it). I vow certain things mutely: I wake at the same time, check the same series of websites in the same order each morning. My breakfast choices are similarly prescribed: eggs and one piece of toast, or cereal, or yogurt and half a banana. Veering is rare. Mute vows are the best; no one needs to know how slavishly I exist.

My day proceeds along the same familiar route. Now that I am back to my full-time teaching schedule, I move briskly through my routine so that no one can see how fragile I feel as I go to class, hold office hours, drive home, let the dog out, do yoga, shower, and prepare dinner.

Sometimes I go out in the evenings to poetry or fiction readings given by friends, but my main focus is on getting through, making my small contribution, then retreating.

There's nothing, on the surface, wrong with this picture. Except that I used to refuse to retreat. I used to crave an uphill battle. Now I favor the groove, disdaining the battle that would mean recovering my previous position—when I was someone at ease, someone who was comfortable in the world. I avoid any disturbances to my routine. I keep surprises at bay.

My strict routine is a talisman against the next unpredictable event that might be the death of me. This impression of control is a false equivalency, but I trust it for now. I will remain in the groove for however long *now* lasts.

CLUTTER

His voice often trickles down the stairs from his bedroom to the kitchen where I am working. Always, it seems, I am in the kitchen working. Today he is asking for help.

Where is my cat tank? Can I borrow your eyes for a second?

Other times he cannot find his bike shorts, his new socks, his rainsuit zipped into its clever mesh bag. Elias's room, his domain, has always been a mess, a tangle of objects scattered across every available surface. It's always been difficult to forge a way across the carpeted floor to the bed. As long as it's been his room—since he was seven years old and we moved to this house—he's been losing something in it: band forms, trumpet music, tuxedo shirt for a concert, CDs, homework, drumsticks.

In all that time, I have been getting after him to clean it up, now. And in all that time he has been making excuses. Eventually, he learned to appease me with a closed door. Eventually, I learned to accept the mess, grudgingly.

So, none of this chaos is new, except that now, after his return home from the hospitals, everything is new. Now his door must remain at least figuratively open. Now he needs me to choose from the closet an appropriately colored dress shirt. (*You have too many*, I would have said before.) We'll sew Braille labels onto all of the tags eventually, but for now he can't tell his clothes apart by touch. He does, however, know his wardrobe intimately, and he gives me detailed instructions: *I want the burnt-orange, slim-fit, Marc Jacobs shirt.* He needs me to watch as he transfers laundry from his floor to baskets so that I can make sure he doesn't leave a lone sock or a T-shirt nestled behind his keyboard. He needs help deciphering which piles of clean laundry belong in which drawers; there is not always a palpable difference in feel between workout clothes, T-shirts, and pants. He needs me to find the tie with the paisley pattern for his upcoming concert, where he will conduct, for the first time post-accident, a high school trumpet ensemble he's been rehearsing a couple of days a week at a school where his friend Peter is the band director.

He can hear so he can conduct. That much is certain, and it belongs in the *good news* column. He told me recently that if hearing had been the sense he'd lost, he would not have wanted to live.

I know he should not need me or be living at home at the age of twenty-four. During the semester of the accident, he was doing observations for the last few undergraduate classes he would need for his music education degree. He was on track to student-teach that upcoming fall semester, then to graduate in December. But the accident forced him to withdraw from those classes, and he will have to retake them later, when he figures out how to be a blind student (if he *can* be a blind student). He will have to postpone student teaching and his hoped-for teaching career, perhaps forever.

I know he should not need me, but what I mean to say is that he should not be blind. He is, so he does need me in simple ways. I am important—or at least my eyes are.

For now, I am okay with this arrangement. Being needed helps me face the fact that he will move out eventually—soon, probably—and live on his own in a world he can only know through touch. He has recently learned there is an apartment available through Vision Loss Resources (VLR) in Minneapolis, where he goes for training several times a week (classes in Braille, cooking, orientation to and navigation of his new world). He could stay in this apartment while he finishes the program—*could* for him translates into *must*. There has to be something in the new, uneven terrain of our lives that I can recognize or embrace.

But I have been thinking about clutter lately, all of its insidious ramifications. On the one hand, I don't care that his room is a mess; it's one familiar landmark in an otherwise strange landscape. My own office desk is similarly scattered: papers, books, sticky notes, pens, and paper clips covering every inch of space—a sign of my active mind, I always say.

On the other hand, clutter is tricky. The word can describe, literally, "a confused multitude of things"—my newly blind son's room, for instance. But it can also indicate an impulse to ignore or cover up, to purposely create interference to avoid facing reality: think white noise, think obfuscation.

I do wonder what prods my son to live within such chaos, though when he was in high school, I didn't: I simply demanded that he clean his room. I was perpetually frustrated by the mess. It seemed to pointedly dismiss or undervalue all I had worked for, all I had tried to teach him. How could he not take care of his own belongings? Couldn't he be more responsible?

Post-accident, I am more accepting—but only because I have to be. To show I am adapting, if only to myself, I consider possible explanations. Maybe his mind could only focus on the big picture before, on his constant movements to and from opportunities to create music. Maybe the details of his life piled up, literally and figuratively, in his head and in his room and became impossible to manage. After all, he'd been diagnosed with ADHD during his junior year of high school.

If any of this had been true then, wouldn't it be even truer—starkly truer—now?

I don't know what's behind the mess. I've never asked, and I am not going to ask now. I am going to keep overlooking it (and overtake the task of managing it) because I can't complain about such a small pebble on the long path of Elias's recovery. I am going to white-out my own desire for neatness so that when I enter the clutter, I can enter his world. There is always going to be something physically in his way now, something blocking his path forward. When I enter the clutter, I am likewise forced to pay attention, to choose my way carefully.

I pay attention now in so many new ways: scanning the house for normal items that have turned disastrous—an edge of folded-over rug, the dishwasher door left open, the kitchen chairs askew, the furniture shifted, books or boots or boxes in the middle of a wide-open floor.

I also scan his face for signs of grief or pain. He remains surprisingly upbeat, grateful that he survived (though this may be just the surface he presents to the world). I share his gratitude, but my sight takes in his scarred left cheek, his permanently dilated pupils—reminders of the accident's toll.

Recently, I entered his room looking for the mysterious rainsuit—which I could visualize clearly, though not where I'd last seen it—and was brought up short by some items in his closet and nightstand: two digital cameras in their neat zipped cases. I could almost remember when Elias had bought them to record events he didn't want to forget. Now they are as inert, as useless, as binoculars are to him. His important moments will have to be captured solely in memory, that capricious storehouse. They can be recorded in sound only, without visual detail.

The discovery of those cameras caught me off guard. I stood still, tamping down the urge to shudder, holding off an avalanche of grief and fury, the main challenges of cheerful acceptance.

The mess in my son's room, the sudden appearance of

random items—none of this surprised me. What surprised me was my reaction, or my refusal to react. As I held the cameras, I halted my flood of emotions. Instead—cocking a hip, casting my eyes toward the window—I considered the picture I was creating: *Fully Functioning Mother Stumbles upon Artifacts That Make Her Crumble.*

But I did not crumble. I paused, lost in a jumble of self-aware concentration. I was both audience and actor, performing a role and watching myself at the same time. I was a substitute Hamlet (though I hesitate to make that comparison), feigning sanity instead of madness. For it might be madness to be caught up so fully, to be mirror to one's own nature, reflecting gestures meant to showcase control and hide disorientation and grief.

I have been thus divided since the night of the accident, when I had to adopt the role of unperturbable mother, collaring my own fear and panic, subduing it. My own and, I believed, my son's survival depended on it. *If I fall apart,* I believed, *my son might die.* This was not a conscious thought, but a hidden piston pumping below my consciousness, keeping my engine running. It allowed me to move carefully to my bedroom to pack, to make my way to my car, to drive three and a half hours to the hospital, to walk toward the elevator, to ascend three floors to a room in the ICU where my son was unaware of my presence. For months after that, it allowed me to hold any body part that was unencumbered, to ask sensible questions of doctors, to refuse despair when the diagnosis of blindness arrived.

That strange logic of surviving trauma prevails still. I have been unable to shake this arranged approach to life. I have watched myself manage my own emotions. I have deployed a white noise of controlled movement to obscure the chaos of feeling that threatens to overwhelm.

Time for anger? *Okay, this five minutes before making dinner should do it. Let it out quickly, then resume the posture of routine.*

Time for despair and regret and one good burst of sheer

frustration? *No, that's too long a meeting, too much to release. Put it on the back burner for now.*

These inner negotiations make me uneasy, though they also help me move through each day, through task after task—a rhythm that soothes, a generated pulse of anticipation. Anyone watching—as I imagine, observing me—would think I am fine. I am holding up. I am managing everything. I have been convincing in my role.

Sometimes, though, I worry that I have gotten stuck, that I have become a mechanical version of the person I used to be, maneuvering through long days, my smile pasted onto my face, my open arms stiff and theatrical, welcoming problems that fit within my scope or circumference. I worry that I sweep across the stage of my life, an unbendable woman insisting on a certain distance—emotion enacted, a performance of the deeply felt. Convincing.

Untouchable.

I want to believe that heaviness and introspection, doubt and fury, and abject helplessness have not forced me to stay this way forever. I want to believe that my ability to experience love and tenderness have not been subsumed by my need to avoid breaking down: a need that once served a vital purpose and maybe still does.

I am not sure what to think. This makes me a foreigner in my own life—I, who have always known what to think.

That day, as afternoon bled away, as I held Elias's cameras in my hand, I was frozen in acutely aware contemplation, surrounded by a scattering of objects so thick I could barely see my path out.

BALANCE

He was just five when he mastered the solo routine on his bike, a steel-blue hand-me-down from Nate. Our street, Fremont Avenue, was under construction in the spring of 1996, so he practiced on graded sandy soil and swaths of dirt without obstruction or traffic. His way would be clear, his landings soft, or so I believed.

I wonder now what it was like to be the youngest of three boys, the baby. Surely we never called him that to his face, yet he must've absorbed his parents' and brothers' doting attitudes from our daily actions.

Do you want a cracker? we'd croon.

Without waiting for his response, we'd hand him a cracker. That was one chorus we sang.

Do you need help?

In response to his silence, we would help him. That was another verse.

He's trying to say. . . . Yet another verse.

Maybe it was our fault that he learned to speak much later than his brothers had.

The bike-riding day, as I remember, was nondescript: sunny, I suppose, and clear, not too warm or cold. It was around his birthday, in the middle of May, the time of year when hope returns, when the harsh cloak of winter is slowly replaced by a lacy light green shawl of burgeoning growth.

We had practiced first in the parking area in our backyard, a flat expanse of blacktop next to the garage with enough space to accommodate at least two cars abreast. Elias was doing fine, pedaling with my help. I was the one who decided he now needed more space, needed to feel his independence.

So we moved to the street in front of the house, where I wanted him to feel his legs propelling him forward over a long stretch of road; where he could build the confidence to pedal on his own, to ride around the block whenever he wished, to expand his world.

On that day of mastery, I ran along behind him, holding onto his bike seat. I don't know how many passes we made back and forth in front of the house, but suddenly he started pedaling differently. I sensed vigor in his motion. Before, I'd been struggling to keep pace with him on the uneven ground. I was running—skidding, really, into uneven trenches—while holding onto his randomly weaving bike. Then the wobbling stopped, and I felt the change through my grip on the seat: he was maintaining his balance while speeding along.

You're doing it! I crowed.

Then I blurted, *I'm letting you go!*

He was the youngest of my three boys, the baby, the one who was supposed to break my heart.

Now he twisted his body halfway around, still pedaling forward, to throw his voice back in my direction. *But not forever?*

I stopped running, suspended in this sticky substance of love. I laughed to myself, but I also felt a pang. How could he think I'd ever let him go for good?

I'm here, buddy! I said in response. Those words were probably not enough to calm his sudden fear. But I was inordinately pleased at his sensitivity. I thought, *How lucky I am to have a child like this, who feels things deeply.*

I savor that moment now, these twenty years later. He'd admitted he needed me, even if he couldn't say it in words.

Tonight, he is almost a year past his life-changing accident. Earlier today, Rich and Kay and I had helped him move into an apartment in a high-rise near downtown Minneapolis. The main purpose of the move was practical: he could be closer to VLR.

It was his spirit of hopefulness and the naïveté of youth that had compelled him to live on his own. But it was also the smothering fact of my presence in the house. He had not blamed me, but his daily world had become too much with me in it. My presence had dampened his prospects for independence.

Naturally. He was a twenty-four-year-old man living with his mother. He said, in exasperation (and I believed him), *I can't be that guy bringing girls to my mom's basement.*

Tonight, I called him at his new place because, after attending an evening meeting, I came home to a house empty of his vibrant presence. He indulged me, confessed that he knew already that living alone in an apartment would be a major adjustment: no friends available at any time of day or night; moments of intense loneliness.

He's going to adjust. We both know that. He's been through so many adjustments in the last year. Clearly, we both know that as well.

In my mind, I traveled back to that shredded roadway where he had learned to balance as I'd urged him forward, where he had learned to be glad for the freedom of a bike ride and aware there's a toll for that freedom.

Except that today the roles are reversed.

Good night, I said, reminding him that I keep my cellphone near my bed every night. *Call me if you need anything. Or if you just want to hear a familiar voice.*

(*Tug, tug*, I implied in my cloying mother way).

Will do, he said, almost, but not quite, dismissing my concern.

In his bland answer I felt a recognition: *I'm the one who's not ready*. It's my voice, thrown behind me into air, shocked at the realization that he's letting me go.

As I hung up, I envisioned him smiling at his newly fashioned independence and pleased with his choice to set me free to do battle with my own sense of balance.

DREAMS

Last night, I wept continually through my dreams, all of which reflected me in positions of loss: husband leaving, children leaving, me leaving. In each dream, there was a moment when I broke down and sobbed, all of my reserves spent on the outpour.

I woke with a slight headache, thinking, *Even when it's fake crying in dreams, it has the same effect as a good cry in life.* Crying wrings energy out of me, leaves me achy and depleted.

But I don't usually cry like that—not in front of people anyway. Elias doesn't spend a lot of time crying or lamenting either. He takes huge steps forward bravely, as when, just six months after the accident, he started his intensive training at VLR in Minneapolis to learn how to read Braille and how to navigate his dark world; as when he started to take Metro Mobility for transportation; as when he decided to move into the available VLR apartment. He forges ahead, in spite of any inner laments.

Because of VLR, he's taken more giant steps forward: cooking, woodworking, riding the city bus on short errands around town. He's learned to navigate well enough to walk to VLR alone from his apartment, a stroll of about a mile that requires him to cross several busy intersections.

How did that go? I asked when he told me recently about those walks. I needed all of my strength to keep my tone even.

I was terrified, he said. And then he paused. *But I did it.*

Having lived on his own now for about two months, he's doing well—better than I am. Yet last night when I spoke to him on the phone before bed, he told me he hadn't gone to VLR that day. I knew he hadn't gone on the previous day, either.

Are you sick? I asked.

No, not really.

I wonder if you're just feeling the effect of it all. I paused. *You know—everything.*

We finished our conversation and hung up, but a few minutes later I texted him to see if he wanted me to pick him up and bring him home—to my house, I meant. I still call it *home*, and he lets me.

I hauled all of that worry with me into sleep: my concern about his new apartment, my knowledge that he's dealing with long stretches of time alone and some inevitable loneliness. Reality is slowly sinking in for him: he can't see; he won't ever be able to see. But that realization isn't the only thing that's sinking in.

Just yesterday, as I was driving, I took a rare moment to look purposefully ahead. For months, my gaze has been trained on the immediate future, not the distant one. During that time, I have needed to see and be buoyed by progress and accomplishments. Keeping anticipation and excitement at the forefront has kept the weight of Elias's long-term prognosis bearable.

Now we have reached a tentative stability. Elias has some independence, a plan to finish his music ed degree. He manages alone, cooking his own meals, doing his own laundry, and battling the normal emotions of young adulthood: the small energizing encounters and the deep unsatisfied longings.

Still, what I dream of for his future has been tempered. He may fall in love and get married, have children, embark on a long and exciting career, interact with loyal and fun friends. But the loss of his sight will ultimately lead to other losses.

Now, when I describe a landscape to him or the actions of another driver, he can recall seeing those things in his sighted life. For example, he's sympathetic when I erupt at another driver who's been offensive or rude; he chuckles at my mild swearing. He can still give me directions because he remembers all the routes we have driven—that we still drive—though he knows this only because I talk incessantly.

But what will happen in five years or ten? His stored memories will fade. Road construction and other spatial changes will alter the familiar, making it unrecognizable. What colors are, what expressions are—his knowledge of these visuals will also fade.

At a stoplight, where these thoughts swept over me in a rush, my eyes suddenly stung with tears. Then the light changed, so I blinked them away, stepped on the gas, and proceeded home to the tasks at hand.

But I carried the crush of these altered dreams into sleep. No wonder I sobbed all night long. Maybe all of the characters in my dreams were versions of me, as dream shrinks like to predict—the burdened and the burdener, the confessor and the hearer, the cheater and the cheated.

Here's what I know. Each day, I fight to hold off despair and discouragement, one stoic hour at a time. In dreams I can let go of control—because dreams are temporary, dissolving, a place without a witness.

ZEROING IN
One-Year Anniversary

We wake on the morning of that day, all of us—parents, brothers, grandparents. The cycle of a year has brought us back. We zero in on the approaching time, the moment, our present bleeding into the past, our now into then—not serious bleeding, just red pinking the delicate whites. Not reliving so much as retrieving from memory the living of it, sharp and full of sense. An alignment, a realization, an acknowledgment.

It is windy today, violently windy. Empty plastic flowerpots lined up against the garage scutter across the lawn, and torrents of dried leaves scratch at the house. The angry voice of the wind rages, rattles windows and casements, then retreats—whispering, preparing for the next onslaught.

How will we endure the day?

Some of us will go to church—will kneel, bow our heads to pray in gusts of gratitude as strong as the wind, knotted up in the weave of a faith that weathers all: faith as warm as a blanket, as substantial, but growing heavier over time. Belief is so burdensome. As the time approaches, faith provides a reminder of what could have been but was not. Prayers grow more fervent, perhaps even venture from gratitude to petition.

What can one ask for besides life?

If you don't know, no need to ask.

Some of us will raise our heads, if not in prayer, then upward toward some idea of safety: to the roof of a house that shelters, though its corners are assailed by the elements. We are seeking, but what we are seeking—that is hard to tell. We will read or work, sweep floors or sweep our hands across our foreheads—in memory, in anticipation of the coming jolt.

Some of us will work, toil as we do each day, having made of ourselves or our contributions or our view of our contributions a figure, an idol that sits on the altar of accomplishment, always in view. We will keep our heads down—*down, down*—raising them only in a fog of recollection that we will not breathe on to clear—some nagging sense that all is not right. (We know it is not.)

Still, the work: the checked-off list, survival of what seems fittest; taking stock of what one does, which often—perhaps too often—equals what one (thinks one) is.

Some of us will watch the clock, as if streamlined attention to time now could make up for glaring ignorance then: the 2 p.m. meeting that unfolded as usual, without any inkling of disaster, of the explosive accident and the encroaching horror. And the afternoon's efficiency, the preparation, all that hustling around in the dark—though we would swear the lights were on, our world illumined, its contours clear, nothing hiding in corners—the day spelling out, as all days seemed to do, *routine, routine, routine.* Then the early evening's tamped excitement, its unknowing cheerful outlook, its glowing, rosy optimism.

Some of us will shudder—but the wind, the wind, we will insist, is vicious today. We feel it through the walls. It seeks out the weak, or the weak-willed, and we aren't so tough (today of all days), so it's just niggling at us, antagonizing, tormenting. We will huddle under a blanket on the couch, intrigued at the power of it—to squeak through this solid house with its insulation, its foundation, its radiating warmth (a mere patina of protection).

Some of us will burrow deeply into our heavy coat of feigned cheerfulness, will crawl into routine so familiar we can hide out in it. We may even get lost, become invisible, though we carry with us our burden of feeling. There are always the convolved lengths of sorrow, wound around with bolts of whatever we need to cover it. The sorrow becomes filling, stuffing—our insides.

All of us will gather for dinner—it is decided—at the precise hour, 6 p.m., when the hands of the clock pointed in opposite directions that day, reminding us that what looks upright, creates a perfect straight line, a fine and flawless figure, can hide the crooked, the flawed, the fateful.

As if we wouldn't remember the time, that evening—not the phone call, not even the usual warning, but the visit: news arriving on foot, followed by the simple gesture of packing. Then minutes—hours?—wracked with dread and uncertainty and hope. The cellphone on the car seat, hands settled on the wheel, tires following a route so familiar we almost forget that we didn't know what would be at the end of the road.

We would find out, though, each in our own time. Each of us would meet the stunning truth, privately and together: our boy, hanging to life by a thread, encased in a web of tubes and sounds whose unfamiliar presence would soon become part of the routine, all of this horror ushering in the wisdom we looked to for hope, the assurance that another day would be ours—would be his.

We will gather tonight, still uncertain, knowing only what's past, what we have moved through and beyond—recalling not each bump and twist over which we've traveled but the past smooth and straight and true. The past points to here, where we gather around a table, forge a circle. We create what holds us, protects us, no matter if the wind shuts the hell up or continues to yammer.

Our breaths will come together to create our own wind, made up of what we bring here, a year on: anger and regret, pride and joy, horror, dismay, hope, or destitution.

The room will be filled with our collective breaths, blowing in various intensities, joined perhaps by the breath of spirit that enlivens the world, whispering *survival*. Not in words. No, words can be saved for later, when in darkened rooms we may bare the bitter truth of persistent anguish. Where and when we gather, no words will be needed.

Presence, which we didn't, couldn't, provide then, didn't even know was missing—our presence here, all of us, will blow us past the memory of the hour we couldn't anticipate.

Presence will still our questions (for now), the wind of the soul that howls in the night its long-drawn-out *why*.

All of us will gather. The gathering will be all. Our boy in the circle with us.

Enough.

IT GROWS DARK

It was 8 p.m. on March 30, 2016, just over a year since the accident. I circulated through my house (*my* house, evidence of a distinct presence in the world), methodically closing blinds and curtains.

It is growing dark, I announced out loud to no one—to myself— expressing the marvel of this season. A month ago, I calculated, I would have been performing this ritual starting at 7 p.m. or 6 p.m.

It was growing dark, and I wondered at the multiple nuances of the word *grow*, glancing at the herb garden I had started in cheap colorful plastic pots near the south-facing kitchen window. The seeds had sprouted; the experiment had worked. Yet I couldn't say I'd succeeded until I could show that I'd kept the shoots growing long enough to plant them outside. I thought, *Maybe I should thin them, maybe apply eggshell fertilizer, maybe talk to them nicely.*

It was growing dark, and I wanted to make sure I knew all the ramifications of growing because I surely knew dark.

It had been so dark on the weekend we'd found out that Elias was blind. We couldn't even see to the next hour.

We'd left him alone in his hospital room—alone!—sedated

(blind), and we'd gone to our hotel rooms to encounter images that intruded as we thrust them out with a violence usually reserved for instinct or combat.

We'd sat in a circle, enclosed—each, all of the family members, in our own darkness, talking about everything we couldn't know, could only imagine. We'd made fantastic predictions: *out of bed soon, back to the gym soon, home soon.* Our conversation was trivial that night. We couldn't begin to know how to conjure words about a whole life lived in darkness.

Grow equals expansion. Yes, light is draining away, receding, but what's left is filling that space. What's left is lack-of-light, plain darkness, which grows more prominent as I write.

Grow also suggests gain. But what is gained by impending, expanding darkness? More blanks. Less sight.

More perspective?

Did I close the blinds to think more clearly? No, I closed them to keep anyone from thinking about what I might be doing in my house, in the dark, on this late winter day. I closed them to keep myself from wondering what's out there, who's out there, what anyone might be doing so close to my house, looking in at my shadow.

I said to myself, *I have grown up. I have grown emotionally. I have grown into a person who can accept failure. I have grown to accept my son's blindness.*

But the growing darkness told me that pronouncements like these were piles of growing bullshit. One would need a public radio–style voice to make that believable (think *Saturday Night Live*, think Ana Gasteyer).

Grow means "to become."

Yes, the process of becoming, as in *I'm becoming a lunatic waiting for morning, for actual spring. I'm living a threadbare existence, babbling infinitives, engaged in contemplation so self-directed it winds toward implosion. I'm becoming someone who tires of pondering what it means that my world is growing darker by the second.*

NOW I KNOW

I have always known only the basic facts of the accident. (I mean, of course, what caused it.):

A drunk driver had been headed the wrong way down Interstate 94.

The driver had traveled the wrong way for as little as half a mile or as much as two miles before the collision.

Elias had been driving in the left lane, his preference, his view obscured by the semis and cars in front of him.

This section of road was on a hill, and that rise—plus the semi-trucks—had obscured his view of the oncoming car.

Only a foot of the Civic's front end had collided with the driver's-side headlight of the drunk driver's Town Car, which meant that Elias had swerved hard to avoid catastrophe.

The Civic had careened away from the impact. It had skidded, flipped over, wound up in a ditch fifty yards or more from the freeway. Parts of it—a bumper, a wheel, tiny pieces of glass—had littered the way.

I have come to know or acknowledge other things that could

be called facts, though they don't relate directly or solely to
this accident:

At seventy miles per hour, it is hard to imagine any impediment
to progress.

At two o'clock in the afternoon, few drivers are thinking of impending disaster.

At high speeds, it is hard to tell in which direction an object is
moving.

At high speeds, drivers often relax, as if they are handling the
only car on the road.

At high speeds, a swerve takes less than half a second, and that
might not be enough time.

For a long time, armed with this information, I swayed safely
in the land of the unimaginative. I don't mean that I was without
imagination, but I was unable to imagine the force of the impact.
I couldn't visualize it—I didn't want to. It seemed impossible—by
which I meant, easy to avoid.

But just yesterday a local news station aired a follow-up story,
an upbeat piece that showcased how far Elias had come in just
over a year. It told how he was back to working with a high school
band again, walking on his own again, talking without the trach
tubing and wiring that had impeded his voice when the same
reporter had met with him for an earlier story.

In the follow-up story, the reporter included a flashback to
the accident scene—for contrast—and clips from some audio
that we hadn't heard before, that we hadn't known existed. As
the TV screen showed still photos of both mangled cars, this
soundtrack played in the background, a way to re-create the
accident scene for viewers who hadn't watched the earlier story
or hadn't understood the severity of the accident.

Layered over the static and the official-sounding voices of the
first responders was the sound of my son's voice screaming or
crying or roaring—an awful unintelligible noise, like an animal

trying to break through some communication barrier and speak.

Twice in the audio clip, this otherworldly, visceral yell: Elias's pure bewildered rage.

I've watched the story twice, and each time I have recoiled, cringing into the depths of my body, at the sound of my son in his extremity of pain and panic and fear.

This is not a sound I would have been able to conjure or imagine.

This is not a sound I am grateful to have heard.

Yet I now know a little more about what the accident was like. I still can't visualize it, but the sound of my son's desperate, furious cry has stirred my gut.

This is what it means to be haunted. I can't unremember that sound.

A few days after the story aired, the reporter called Elias to apologize for not letting him know about the audio clips ahead of time.

He is a decent man, genuinely moved by my son's story and gracious attitude; he wanted to share Elias's outlook with others—hence the followup story. He said, when Elias asked, that the audio had come from a video recording that someone—the state trooper, probably—had taken at the scene of the accident.

What this means is that somewhere, in a police officer's desk drawer, in a file cabinet at state patrol headquarters, on someone's computer, are pictures of my son in his mangled car, bleeding and frantic and nearly out of his mind with confusion and pain. There are images to go with the sound.

There may be footage of his compound fracture, radius and ulna protruding from his left forearm: a picture of his actual bones exposed to air. There may be pictures of glass in his eyes or, after they cut his clothing off, in the skin of his chest, shoulders, and arms. There may be images of blood flowing from places I saw only after they had been cleaned, stitched, bandaged.

Firefighters may have been filmed picking out the glass carefully, as if they were playing Operation. There may be more sounds, an image of Elias struggling to speak. (Though his jaw was broken, firefighters said he told them his name and birthdate.) Or, worse, there may be a voice I can't recognize, one strained by the torment of the accident.

There would have been blood flowing into his mouth, a scene from a kind of mockumentary horror film, maybe a gurgle instead of words. There may be a record of sounds and images worse than these.

I don't want that record in the world.

I thought the ultimate loss of control was to recognize that I couldn't have prevented the accident. Now I know I was wrong.

GREEN BEANS

After neglecting my garden for a season—*neglect* may be too strong a word—I planted again, just over a year after the accident.

In one section I have two rows of green beans. I planted the seeds more or less as the package directed, pushing an index finger into the soil at semiregular intervals along the length of twine I used for a row marker, then dropping a kidney-shaped seed into each hole, covering it up, hoping for the best.

Despite crowding (I doubted the wisdom of the suggested spacing), my plants curled into life. My bean garden, a sliver of my full garden, was successful. Not everything survived, but I cultivated nine or ten robust plants.

There's something about green beans that makes me dither. Even the bush variety could benefit from staking, though the seed package doesn't suggest it. But I tend not to stake them, making my job of picking more difficult. Last time I planted, also a year when I didn't prop up the beans, I didn't see any fruit until many of the pods were grown too fat to enjoy. Nothing tastes worse than an overgrown green bean. Then I hastily picked, but the entire crop was affected. The plants petered out from lack of stimulation.

This year, when I woke each morning in early June, I imagined myself, armed with twine and a couple of stakes, bringing order to the chaos that my bean rows were becoming, providing them with ropes to lean on, like prizefighters. However, I found it difficult to rouse myself from early morning dreams, much less foster any real change in my gardens. I never staked the beans.

Instead, I decided to pick early and often, leaving the leafy, floppy plants to their own wise devices. Starting in early July, each day I gently lifted the plants and searched for the ripe fruit. (Elias was moving from his VLR apartment to his own townhouse that summer, sixteen months after the accident, against my better judgment.)

I was thrilled that my plants were producing. I kept a Ziploc bag of fresh beans in my refrigerator's produce drawer. At least once a week, I steamed or roasted them for dinner, adding a pinch of salt, a dash of pepper, a lump of butter. They were delicious: crisp, sweet, squeaky, as fresh green beans should be.

One day, after a riotous August thunderstorm, I noticed that strong winds had torn one plant out of the ground. It lay on its side, a pile of potential, inert. I ignored it at first, too lazy to carry it to its compost grave, focusing instead on the seven or eight plants still thriving, still laden with fruit.

Finally, after about a week, I exerted myself to remove the defunct vine. I found, to my surprise, that it was still alive. It should have been as light as twine, but instead I found myself tugging. The plant was attached to earth by a rope of fibers. Lifting the mass of leaves, I discovered a cache of plump beans hidden underneath, ready for harvest.

Since then, vigilantly but with requisite caution, I have lifted the dying arms each day to harvest beans in the last days of this heroism.

(My son does his own dishes and laundry. He tells me he's not afraid to live alone in his townhouse. *What if there is a fire*, I ask? *Mom, if there is a fire, I'll sense it and jump out of my bedroom window.*)

As for the other healthy plants, I pick cursorily. This one receives my special attention. So far, it has produced beyond its means. It lies, still, in a gesture of surrender but continues to multiply, tethered stubbornly to soil by its thin root.

It is negligible, capable of being thrashed around like a pom-pom. This is enough mystery to keep me returning to the garden.

(Elias offers to make me a sandwich when I visit him in his new home, a strange and strangely pleasant reversal of roles.)

I don't admire the plant itself but the plant's commitment. Each day, it defies odds. It tugs and burdens, keeps me moving forward with anticipation.

BACKSTORY

I have always loved a good backstory. Lives both fictional and actual make more sense when I know their past circumstances. When Ophelia kills herself in *Hamlet*, any viewer can see what has contributed to her decision: she's been traded like currency among the men in her life, used as bait and worse; her affection and loyalty have been plundered. When her father dies at the hands of her former crush, something breaks in her; she goes mad, and that madness escorts her to suicide. Years ago, I was so compelled by her story that I wrote a series of poems in her voice.

When Nate ran a race with me on Thanksgiving Day of 2016, his reaction showcased the idea of backstory. He was worried about the presence of terrorists at this less than noteworthy event. (We had paid our entry fee with canned goods.) As he ran, he constantly turned his head from side to side, scanning the crowds along the route for any hint of danger. His anxiety had been primed by a year spent in Iraq during that second disastrous war. As a radar specialist, his survival and the survival of his unit had depended on constant vigilance. Even though he was home now, his vigilance remained, a remnant he couldn't shrug off like a jacket.

But what is the backstory of an unforeseen event, a tragedy? In court, when I heard that the driver who'd rammed my son's vehicle at seventy miles per hour because she was drunk at 2 p.m. on a Monday and speeding the wrong way down the interstate, I didn't care what had led to her decision. I didn't care, but her backstory came tumbling out anyway, as if she were obeying an impulse so strong she couldn't withstand it.

She had struggled for twenty years with addiction.

She had been sober for two months prior to the accident.

On the day of the accident, she said, she'd come home from a Zumba class and started drinking tequila.

Why Zumba? I wondered. (Who could formulate an answer to that question?)

Why tequila? That I can guess—shots thrown back, the easiest way to a quick numbing.

She'd gone blank and could remember nothing else after that.

Her story—not a story, really, just a collection of facts—sounded scripted to me, something that could have been written by any alcoholic or drug addict. Because of that, it didn't have the power to move me or offer satisfaction. It made the driver seem one-dimensional, a stock character in a stock tale, all of the details utterly predictable.

People like her, I thought, *say "I'm sorry," pause, then hit repeat.* Did she ever tell Elias directly that she was sorry? I can't remember.

What I do remember is that many of the family gathered at the courthouse for her sentencing hearing that day read victim impact statements. Nate, his voice quivering, shared that, when serving in Iraq, he had never really been scared. But when he'd seen Elias in the hospital after the accident, he'd been terrified.

My sister Terri wrote eloquently. She couldn't be there, so someone else read her statement to the court. Yes, she wrote, it was a miracle that Elias had survived, but he had paid a price for that miracle: *He will never look into the sparkling eyes of the woman who is captivated by his kindness, confidence, and sense of humor. He will not be able to see the joy in her eyes when he proposes.*

I spoke of what I had lost: *my faith in justice, a sense that the world and its people are fundamentally good. A sense of balance. An abiding trust in the ordinary and routine.* But Elias—well, Elias moved us all to tears.

He pleaded for the judge not merely to sentence this woman to jail but to put mechanisms into place that would prompt her to stay sober: to sentence her to a probation period that would prohibit her from public bars so she would be more inclined to stay sober, to require her to speak to groups of high school students or Mothers against Drunk Driving groups so that another person might avoid doing what she had done. If she could be required to do these positive things, he said, then something good might come out of something bad. Maybe she could be transformed, not forever defined by the past. Her backstory could be transformed; that's how I saw it.

As proud of him as I was that day, I also considered my son's backstory, the counterweight to the story the other driver had blurted out. In the big-picture sense, he had been about to graduate from college. For years he had been teaching high school students to drum. In a narrower sense, he was returning home from a routine visit to Fargo, anticipating a late-afternoon get-together with a friend. He meant to go to work the next day, finish his teaching observations, enroll in one final education class for the summer, student-teach in the fall, graduate at Christmas. He meant to move steadily toward his main passion: working with high school students in band, drumline, marching band. Did any of this matter anymore?

His backstory had nothing to do with the accident. Instead, it terminated in the irrevocable fact of the accident. The life he had been preparing for had disappeared in a hail of glass and debris. Unlike the other driver, who would resume—even with required jail time and community service—a life similar to the one she had been living before the accident. That would never be possible for Elias.

The accident, the accident. We were forced, from a single random moment in time, to refer forever after to *the accident.* Usually, that word means no one is at fault; it means something couldn't have been prevented. Those shots of tequila may have been the only part of the accident—our accident, Elias's accident—that literally qualified as accident. They signified a mistake, a brief lapse of will. But to me, picking up keys and opening a car door and turning a key in the ignition and backing into the road are all decisions—impaired, yes—that anyone with a history of drinking knows in some stubborn, subconscious part of the mind to be bad ideas.

This accident had replaced Elias's old ambitious, promising backstory. It had become his new backstory. His demonstrations of courage and sympathy, his stubborn refusal to feel sorry for himself made it clear that he would proceed with his life gratefully, irrepressibly; that he would not let a moment redefine him. His life would be different on the surface, but his core would remain the same.

How could I not be grateful for his attitude? I was. I am. But the accident has caused me to struggle with my senses and my tenses. Some things can only be expressed in the past tense: *I wanted to see Elias direct his first high school band concert.* Some things that I express in the present tense—because I can't help it—are fruitless desires. I want the film to rewind. I want the driver to stay home and enjoy her tequila or to realize her mistake and pull onto the shoulder and weep with relief. I want Elias to change his plans—to uncharacteristically blow off work or class, to stay an extra day in Fargo, and therefore to arrive home safely, ignoring me as he moves past my outstretched arms, hurrying forward toward his future, the stuff of his wildest dreams.

But Elias can't—couldn't—shake his resolve, divert his attention from the necessary. His backstory was, and still is, simply his story: to drive forward toward his future (ha ha, *drive*), confronting whatever stands in his way.

But he may never. We may never.

He can't see, none of us can see, the final outcome of this outrageous fortune.

PART III

ORDINARY

Almost two years after the accident, Elias and I—or I should say *I*—parked the car and made our way toward the entrance of the palatial Hy-Vee grocery store that had recently opened near his townhome. The parking lot was carpeted in slush, and we walked slowly—slogged, even. Our conversation, begun in the car, continued to unspool.

You give up so easily, he said.

No, I don't!

Yes, you do. But not over big things, he conceded.

Yes? I paused, hoping for clarification.

Okay. Remember Costco? We couldn't find the milk, so you decided they didn't carry it anymore.

But I didn't actually say it!

Yes, you did.

No, I didn't. Maybe I did—I thought about it. But then I remembered the dairy room, and we went there and found your milk.

I laughed, a little uneasy. By now we had entered the cavernous Hy-Vee, and I had accessed his shopping list on his iPhone and was calculating the most efficient route through this store that was new to me.

I didn't know which way to turn. We paused in the produce section, near the takeout-food section, but I couldn't tell what was beyond the cheese cases I could see up ahead. I was flustered, trying to navigate without seeming lost, trying to keep our conversation going at the same time.

You pick on me all the time, I couldn't help saying, casting my eyes back and forth, calculating my position in the store.

I do, he admitted. *You're such an easy target. You just put it out there, and I can't resist.*

I shrugged off his comment. I knew I was no match for his wit—surely not now, as I steered our cart toward whatever was beyond the produce section, preoccupied with his list.

Our conversation, to any other shopper, would have sounded normal: idle, garden-variety, occasionally intriguing chatter overheard while steering a cart down a grocery aisle; talk meant to be ignored. We looked like an average mother-and-son combo, complete with repartee. He was taller and sturdier than me, though, in my mid-fifties, I certainly wasn't decrepit. I was strong and young-looking (I hoped), gray-haired (but not completely), fairly lean. What could be wrong with this picture?

What was wrong was that Elias was almost twenty-six years old, blind, and shopping with his mother. He walked next to me, gripping the cart with his left hand as I navigated the labyrinthine aisles, trying not to run him into a display of Cheerios.

In public situations such as this one, I usually managed to display a casual acceptance of our situation—his situation, I mean. I smiled at other shoppers, trying to ward off their pitying glances. I piloted us confidently from one aisle to the next, though I was only pretending that I knew where I was going.

See, we're fine, my posture broadcast.

Don't stare, my averted eyes begged.

How many times a day did I use the words *see* or *saw, sight* or *image* in normal conversation?

Often. Always.

Elias's quick reactions and witty comments—including those directed at me—were one source of the ordinary in our post-accident lives. He had always delighted in pushing me to my limits, constantly trying to get a rise out of me. That had not changed. He'd had a long history of pronouncing words wrong so that I would correct him, so that he could keep repeating the incorrect pronunciation, so that he could force me to keep saying, *No, it's pronounced el-o-CU-shun.* He'd kept up that practice after the accident. Wasn't I grateful for that familiar behavior?

As we traversed the Hy-Vee aisles, we looked ordinary. I might have even believed we *were* ordinary because we created such a convincing surface. That surface—our camaraderie, our obvious familial resemblance—proved that he was the same son he had always been, despite everything.

But my surging gratitude receded quickly when I remembered that he was not the same, not really. Before, he'd always looked over my shoulder as I'd played solitaire on the computer, pointing out all the moves I'd missed. When I played the game at home now, I missed his once-annoying input: *Didn't you see that? You should have moved that queen over to the king of clubs.* His hand would rest on my shoulder as he leaned over, rather than on my elbow, as it must now.

And I remembered all those years he'd spent helping me improve the yard, designing and building several raised garden beds, paving a small area next to the garage for the garbage and recycling bins. He'd been full of ideas, then.

Here's what you should do: extend these paving stones all the way down the driveway to the street, he'd say. Or *Take out all this edging and replace it and expand this garden area—nothing grows under that crab tree anyway.*

I recalled—though I ached to recall—the many times he'd breezed in from work, tossed his car keys onto the counter, asked if I could make him a sandwich while he changed clothes before heading to the gym.

His sight could outpace mine. I'd accepted his superior vision as ordinary, and I'd benefited from it in practical ways.

Now we have redefined *ordinary*, recalculated benefits—as we are forced to do with everything else in our lives.

INVISIBLE

Out of the blue, Elias announced casually, while we were driving somewhere (always, always, the difficult truths surface when we are driving somewhere), *Mom, you need to see Dan.*

Dan is his therapist.

I was taking Elias to some appointment, and I was caught off guard at this seemingly unprompted remark.

More than anything, I was indignant. If Elias had not been blind, I would have retaliated: *How dare you tell me I need therapy?* But I recognized the drama of such a response, and I refrained. The accident had added enough drama to our lives, his life. Our scenery had changed, and so had our props. Also, facts are facts, and I had formed my opinion about them—namely, that I would protect my son from emotional highs and lows whenever possible.

He was silent, waiting for me to speak—waiting to catch me in a mistake, I was sure. So I huffed out an answer: *For your information, I already have a therapist.*

You do? His surprise was swift, and that made it rough; it rubbed me the wrong way.

Yes, I do, I said. *I've been seeing her for over eight months.*

How had he not known this? Hadn't I mentioned it? Even if I hadn't, his sight in all other areas beyond vision was better than it had been before the accident.

I had started seeing J__ in November 2016, just before Thanksgiving, a year and a half after the accident. It was now late 2017. But why was I asserting these facts to myself? Did I need to verbally establish this timeline to defend myself?

We were silent, both of us mulling possible responses. Needles of indignation pricked my fingers as they clutched the steering wheel. I sat in the heat of my embarrassment: he'd put me on the spot.

When the silence became uncomfortable, I finally broke it. In an even tone, I hoped, I asked, *Just out of curiosity, what makes you say I need a therapist?*

You're stressed out all the time! he blurted. *Or*—he corrected himself—*you get stressed out more easily than you used to.*

He paused. *It's been going on for more than a year.*

He paused again. *Maybe close to two years.*

You mean since the accident? I offered.

Silence from his corner of the front seat.

I wanted to say, *Cut me some slack,* but I was assaulted by another thought: I had been exposed. That was the real issue.

I had believed that I had been keeping my difficulties to myself, that my therapist had helped me work on my personal challenges alone, in a secluded way. I had convinced myself that those challenges, and my efforts to transcend them, were invisible to him.

Later, I would laugh about our conversation: my son's acute perceptions, my touchy defensiveness.

We were transparent to each other, willingly or not: both of us were see-through.

I reserved the right to define *see* however I wanted.

IN THE CAR ALONE

I still love to drive, despite the accident. No one is more surprised than I am at this fact.

I have never stopped loving it: not in the several months after the accident, when I cruised back and forth between the hotel or my home and the hospitals, comfortable in a routine; not after Elias's release from the hospital, when I ferried him regularly to all of his appointments; not several years later, when I drive by myself, ferrying no one.

That may be because I'm always a better driver than a passenger. I feel at home behind the wheel, comfortable and confident.

I sometimes weave impatiently in and out of traffic, though I am careful, not aggressive. My impatience leads me to keep up a steady dialogue with other drivers, which keeps my actions in check:

Oh, so you're going to pull out in front of me. Try using your blinker, won't you?

Can't we at least go the speed limit?

Dickhead!

Put your goddamn phone away.

Go ahead and pass me if it makes you feel better.

My roaming eyes take in scenery, billboards, the vista: the big picture. I'm proud of what I remember from high school driver's ed class: always check side mirrors, rearview mirror, out front, looking for obstacles, anything that appears in your 360-degree view.

I may be an impatient driver these days, but I'm not an anxious one. I love the idea of movement in my life. Multiple possibilities always lie ahead, including the as-yet-unrealized future, which always excites me. I recall some lines from Wordsworth about this sense of anticipation: "effort and expectation and desire, and something evermore about to be."[6] That something keeps me focused on the road, focused on simple calculations of distance and time, possible alternate routes, anticipation of whatever I'm headed toward: food, friends, writing, my sons. Whatever it is, it propels me toward what I look forward to, what I can visualize.

However, sometimes my confidence wavers. Sometimes a glint of pink sunset off my rearview mirror confuses me. Sometimes, passing a semitruck, my fingers grip the steering wheel with a strength out of proportion to the danger. Sometimes the cushion of sufficiency I've wrapped around myself loosens, and I flinch at what I rarely consider: Elias at the moment of impact.

I can't, even now, imagine the crash, but my body still reacts, mostly from trying not to picture his body: his broken bones, torn flesh, blood loss—all of those injuries that happened in a moment, a split second; that happened without his preparation or understanding—all of those injuries that landed him in hospitals for three months.

How can I picture my son, spinning out of control, flipping over, screaming in a hail of broken glass and flying objects? Sometimes I think, *If I picture it, I will cause him to relive it, and maybe this time he won't be so lucky.*

He will never be able to picture his future again. Images still lodged in memory will slowly flake and disintegrate, become mere sounds and sensations from the past: like hints of lemon or basil on the tongue; like the sound of his keys, as he tossed them, hitting the counter; like the sight of my face, welcoming him home.

He has new sensations to remember and file away: the texture of the skin on my elbow, which he encircles lightly with his fingers; the chorus of noises that seem to rise out of nowhere in a crowd, that surround him with words minus illustrations and also help him calculate the dimensions of a room or space; the feeling of being always a passenger, someone who can't look through a window to orient himself.

So sometimes, in the bubble of atmosphere inside my car, I exhale slowly, suppressing a shudder, still performing all of the usual safety gestures that are so familiar. My body doesn't slump—never—but something internal gives way, unshapes itself, sags around the edges.

Heaviness and introspection have their momentary way with me. The car is so private, after all. Inside my vehicle, air blows across my body, and no one is checking my face for signs of doubt, or fury, or grief.

PHONE CALLS

Recently, I requested Elias's full hospital records from Sanford Medical Center in Fargo. It was now nearly three years after the accident. I had put off making this request for more than two and a half years, telling myself, when I considered it, that it would still be too difficult for my son to absorb all of the details of that fateful night.

Of course, I am talking about the son who graduated from VLR in less than a year, far ahead of schedule; who told a reporter just months after the accident, *It's not that bad being blind.*

My justification didn't hold up. Though he obviously didn't remember any details of that night, Elias had shown resilience in a thousand ways; he had moved forward admirably, unflappable.

Obviously, it wasn't him I had been protecting. That I was just now ready to request the full report seemed suspect. What was I worried about discovering?

When the flash drive with the records arrived in the mail, I invited Elias over for the viewing.

There won't be anything surprising, but I'll come if you want, he said, with the confidence of someone who wears comfort as a second skin.

You're right, I said (though I had my doubts). I offered to feed him dinner and buy him hard cider—not quite a bribe, but almost.

I didn't realize this until I had the records, but what I specifically wanted to find out was how many times he had been brought back from the brink of death on the night of the accident. In the early months after the accident, he'd often told people that he had literally died in the ER, I guess because someone had told him—a nurse, probably—that he had been revived several times that night.

Years after the event, I wanted a clear view of what I had not witnessed because I needed to answer an important question: was the story we'd been told, or the story my son imagined he'd been told, the real story? I wanted to see the facts in writing: *resuscitated in ER three times.*

After we ate dinner—a meal I have since forgotten—I inserted the flash drive into the USB port on my computer, and we settled down to our reconnaissance. What we saw together—what I read to my son—was both more mundane and more horrifying than what we both—I imagine—had imagined.

There was a large hand-drawn chart among the first forty or so pages of ER records. On it, health care workers had recorded Elias's vital signs every fifteen minutes, from the time he'd arrived at Sanford to the time he was transferred to the ICU, nearly six hours later.

Charts are by nature mundane; only variations draw notice. Hence, we discovered that, at one point, within the space of fifteen minutes, his blood pressure had dropped from about 110/70 (astoundingly normal considering the trauma) to 70/30 (dangerously low). We paused to discuss this information and decided that his body had suddenly, albeit belatedly, adjusted to the facts of the accident and responded: *Holy shit, I'm really hurt, and I've lost a lot of blood.*

Piecing together information from different pages—the records were not tidily arranged—we made a story out of the disparate details. When Elias's blood pressure had dropped, he'd been resuscitated first and then transfused. (This resuscitation was his first "death.") A random note in the chart recorded a *cardiac event,* which we connected to the crashing vitals and subsequent transfusion.

Somewhere during that time—though the time was not clearly delineated in the notes—he'd received six units of blood, plus more units of plasma and red blood cells.

The human body contains between eight and ten pints of blood, I reasoned; each unit of blood is roughly equivalent to one pint. That means, I told myself—incredulously—he'd lost more than 60 percent of his blood that night. (I calculated again, trying to process this information: $6/8$ is $3/4$—closer to 75 percent.)

What was most horrifying about this information was the straightforward way in which it was recorded in Elias's records. Sterile terms were used to describe my son's near-death experience: *sent to IR* (shorthand for *interventional radiology*—we had to look it up) *for transfusion before proceeding to radiology for CT scan.*

These details were recorded matter-of-factly, as if they were part of a normal process, a routine night in the ER. Did anyone wonder, as I did when reading the notes, whether the CT scan would be necessary? If Elias hadn't survived, would it have mattered if a scan had revealed a brain injury?

There were other interesting (that is, difficult) parts as well, such as descriptions of his bleeding: where his blood was erupting, how much was spouting, how he'd reacted.

Mostly, the notes said, he'd remained conscious (a truth that even now I wish I didn't know). He'd kept trying to talk, it seems, to provide medical staff with information they'd requested. (He was trying to be helpful, even in this extremity.) Apparently, he'd given permission for several medical procedures that night. One note said, *Patient says he understands procedure and gives permission.* That note was about inserting some balloons into his nose, which was broken, to stop the bleeding.

I almost laughed out loud when I read that, except that it was not funny. Elias had no recollection of giving permission for this procedure, much less any memory of being aware of his overall condition. He'd been in shock; hadn't any medical personnel recognized that?

Mostly, as we gathered from the charts, blood seemed to have been filling his mouth. Other wounds, such as the deep gashes on his left leg and cheek, the glass shards embedded everywhere, were easier to deal with. External wounds respond well to pressure and patience. But the mouth can be a horror. It had kept filling, and he'd kept spitting blood, then vomiting when he couldn't spit fast enough.

As I read this information, I spasmed involuntarily, my body withdrawing from this reality. His facial bones had all been broken. The effort to vomit must have knocked him back in pain. There were no notes about how *his* body had reacted, as if no one had noticed—or maybe they had noticed, but those details had not been important. Yet there were notes about the volume of his emissions, which meant that it had been someone's job to measure and record those amounts.

Until tonight, I had not thought to picture him—how to picture him—on that far-distant night: not the copious amounts of blood his body had shed nor the various methods for keeping it from choking him—certainly not his awareness of his own bleeding nor his repeated attempts to communicate (which is why, I guess, they'd kept asking his permission).

The reason for this irony, of course, was that I was not there to give permission. I should have been there. Never had my absence seemed more significant. Never had my ignorance of my son's bloody trauma been so visible.

I was taken aback, newly guilty, at the information in these notes. I had believed that my agony was over, but I was wracked with reborn regret that night.

Something else emerged from our reading of all of these data: a clearer picture of my response to news of the accident that night. Once we had finished reviewing the records, I closed the file, removed the memory stick from the computer. Then I turned to my son, sitting in a folding chair by my side, and spoke. *I had no idea how bad it was for you. I couldn't imagine it, but I feel like I should have known.*

We tried to assemble a coherent narrative out of the puzzle pieces of memory, but he still remembered nothing of that night. I remembered mostly an uneventful car ride and an overwhelming, pulsing anticipation driving away all possibility of serious trauma.

When I'd gotten into my car and pointed it toward Fargo, I'd been coiled and ready. Taking action had lent me an energy that kept my nerves on alert, my fear at bay. In addition, the list of injuries I'd written down had calmed me: *Not as bad as it could have been.*

My recollection of the drive itself was hazy. I remembered I was avidly on the lookout for deer plunging up from the ditch—as if I could avoid them—as I was barreling down the highway.

Now, continuing to face Elias, I reported, *As for the reality of your condition, I participated in excessively optimistic conversations with a variety of people for the whole drive.*

I had never shared the details of *my* experience that night with him, so I gave him the rundown in detail.

The first time my phone had rung, I was less than thirty miles from home. I'd picked it up immediately, surprised.

Hi, I'm Alma. The caller was an old friend of Elias's from high school. She wanted me to know that she had posted information about the accident on Facebook; she hoped I wouldn't mind.

In fact, I was relieved. I didn't even have the phone number of Elias's girlfriend at the time. Alma lived in Fargo with her husband and two small children. Could she help? She offered to come to the hospital, run errands—anything we needed. I thanked her, but I couldn't envision that kind of need.

Then my two sisters called. My older sister called first, I think—returning my call, I guess—responding to a short voicemail I had left saying I couldn't play in our scheduled volleyball match that night. I gave her what details I could: accident—can't play tonight—will keep you posted. We stayed on the phone only long enough for her to say she'd get to Fargo soon.

My younger sister also called, offered to drive to Fargo to be with me that night. We talked, by comparison, for a long time. She didn't want me to be alone.

My younger sister suffers from chronic illness, so she would have known some of the demands of hospitalization: the waiting and the uncertainty. But while I understood her and appreciated her offer, I politely declined. The long drive and the effort it would have cost her was more than I was willing to ask. I would be fine on my own.

Tim called later, responding to my earlier voicemail. He had discovered in the interim—an investigation I'd never thought to undertake—that the other driver, the one who'd been going the wrong way down the interstate, was drunk.

This news was a revelation, though not one I could concentrate on at the time. Because of his discovery he was, perhaps, more panicked than I was. I was focused on my son, without excess energy to expend on anger or blame.

Then my mom called, wondering if she should come home early from an annual golf trip. I discouraged it.

Wait until I know more, I said, ever the optimist.

I believe that Nate and Caleb called me, too, though I am less sure of this. That I can't remember whether I talked to my own children that night is a strange jolt to the system, even three years later.

Elias's best friend Jared also called that night. I did remember this conversation, I told Elias. I remembered seeing his name—his number was programmed into my phone—so I picked it up right away.

Jared, my son! I blurted, my usual greeting.

Before I could stop myself, I also blurted, *How are you?*

He emitted a strained chuckle—half gasp—enough for me to realize that I sounded crazy. He had called to ask *me* how I was.

There was a veritable party in my car. Time ticked by innocently. When I was not talking on the phone, I was listening to music while leaning forward and urging time to go faster or speaking out loud to my son: *I'm on the way. I'll be there soon.*

The final chapter of the story I related to Elias was short. At approximately 9 p.m., while I was pumping gas in Detroit Lakes, his ICU nurse called. She wanted to keep me updated, she said: to let me know that a procedure to stop some peripheral blood loss had been done—a carotid embolization.

The procedure seems to have worked, she reported.

While I was listening to her, I was also watching the pump, noting how many gallons of gas my car required to fill the tank. I was absently wondering how she had gotten my cellphone number, too. I didn't remember giving it to anyone at the hospital.

After she had shared her update, she asked, *When do you think you might be here?*

I was so excited about arriving that I read nothing into her question. I had only forty miles to go—that's all I thought about. I told her as much.

After I finished telling this tale, Elias and I sat near my computer and breathed together, heavily, audibly. Then he said, *That nurse called you because she thought I was going to die. She wanted to see if you would get there in time.*

I see that now, I said. *She met me at the elevator door too*, I recalled, though that night I'd thought she was just being friendly.

Now, several years later, these memories tilt me. The accident is long past, but it carries a peculiar power; it can take me back to an old scene in a new way.

I recall what happened that night, but this new knowledge shades what I thought of it both now and then. It seems to change both the present and the past.

Now, for the first time, I fear for my son's life that night.

TRAUMA

Though he never experienced flashbacks of the accident, several years afterward Elias did begin to recall his dreams—not dreams as in sleep-dreams but dreams of what he saw (or imagined he saw?) when he was heavily sedated in the early weeks of his hospital stays.

He remembered a lot, as it turned out, though *remembered* is a loose term.

As we reminisced, I told him that, within two days after the accident, he'd seemed to be responding to us fully, recognizing his dad and me, understanding where he was and what was happening—at least, that's what we'd believed.

I told him how, several days into his stay in the ICU, we'd found him struggling to get out of bed. I could barely pry the gripping fingers of his right hand from the mattress. My story made him recall a vague early memory of trying to move a tremendous, and tremendously heavy, statue of a bull.

Did our memories match up?

I mentioned that, less than two weeks after the accident, he'd seemed fully himself, sitting up in bed, responding to conversations on Saturday, March 28—my birthday—with jolly thumbs-up signs. He was all energy, as if he had swum up from the bottom of the ocean and was overwhelmed by the joy of breathing air—which he was, clearly, now that he was breathing through the inserted O-ring.

He remembered something slightly different: he remembered that my sisters had been there, along with his best friend, his brothers, his grandparents. But he'd thought that we were all at a cabin in northern Minnesota, on a grand vacation together.

Occasionally, in the early days, he'd thought that he was in the back of a food truck and that all of us who were present were trying to help him start a business. This must have been before he'd rediscovered hunger, before he'd starting demanding that extra calories be sent through the feeding tube into his stomach—a small consolation, though Regency hospital staff, doubting his cognizance, had denied him this simple desire for a while. (He'd starved for his truth in those days.)

In a different memory, he recalled voices—someone saying, *You're going to be all right.* Oddly, it was raining in that memory, but the rest of its events seemed unrelated to one another: he thought he was being interviewed outside at a soccer field by his stepbrother Tyler, who had seemed to work for ESPN.

But, no lie, it had been misting on the day of the accident.

The soothing voices he recalled had probably belonged to the paramedics who had rescued him. In the truest version of reality, he'd still been trapped in the wreckage of a car, unable to move his legs.

But what is reality if not what we can conjure up, what we can believe?

Elias seemed to remember the moment when Rich and I had told him he was blind. He recalled being sad for a few minutes. Then the painkillers had slipped him back into a comfortable haze.

I thought, "It's no big deal," he'd said.

None of us had known at the time that he was living in an

alternate reality. Should we have known? The surface had seemed so convincing, so literal. When we'd thought he was rising above, interacting with us in full awareness of his situation, he'd often been hallucinating.

He certainly didn't remember his body as a foreign entity in a bed designed to keep him alienated, off-kilter—thank God. Every fifteen minutes or so, someone—a nurse or a parent— had hoisted up his inert form so that he wouldn't slump, cave in on himself.

No wonder, these three years since, our memories don't match up. No wonder I shake my head sadly, trying to piece these different realities together.

How clouded was my understanding, how deep my longing to believe what I wanted to be true.

CUTTING WORDS

You know, he began, *an older person—someone in worse physical condition—wouldn't have survived.*

Yes? I said, hesitant to pursue this line of thinking.

It's better that it happened to me. I was strong and in good shape, so I didn't die. Someone else would have died.

We were seated in his therapist's waiting room, settled into vinyl armchairs, hemmed in by a closed door on one side and a small water cooler and white-noise machine on the other. We had barely made it up the stairs.

You sound like you're saying you're glad it happened to you? I offered. I was trying to sound neutral, but my statement came out as a question.

As soon as we'd entered the building that day, I'd realized: no elevator. I ought to have remembered this fact, given that Dan had been my sons' therapist for years and had saved at least one of their lives. Instead, confused and ignorant, I'd pushed Elias in his wheelchair to the foot of the stairs, suddenly defeated.

Can we do this? I'd asked. *Do you want to reschedule?*

I'd felt worse than stupid. We were barely two months

post-accident, and it had been my idea to start therapy. Elias had been ready to talk, but now we had no way to get him to the second floor to meet his therapist. He'd been taking a few steps at a time recently, from his bed to a chair in his hospital room but, after months in bed, he had little strength to spare.

No, I'll just use the stairs.

I'd helped him stand and pivot, then lower his butt onto the bottom step. Next, he'd hoisted himself upward, using his good right arm and pushing with both his legs, one painful step at a time, all the way to the top. I'd climbed behind, carrying the folded wheelchair.

We'd made it. He'd made it, I mean.

Resting in our chairs, we were chatting, waiting for the appointment. We had no life outside recovery, so we were discussing the accident and its aftermath.

He was upbeat that day, maybe because of the triumph of the stairs. As we waited, we recalled details of his salvation at the hands of many, the impeccable timing of it all. The first bystanders on the scene (one of them an EMT) had removed the windshield so his bleeding would slow down in the cool March air. The first responders had extracted him from the car in less than twenty minutes. The helicopter transport that the state trooper had already called was waiting to get him to the hospital quickly. Everything had lined up perfectly. Maybe the miracle was simple: his life had been saved by good timing.

But when he casually suggested that it had been better for him to have been struck down than for someone else, our conversation turned serious.

That's hard for me to hear, I said.

I know.

This honesty, this getting to the truth fearlessly, was one gift during a period of much challenge. He and I experienced thrillingly deep, intimate conversations almost daily—every parent's dream. But I was not thrilled to hear this.

When the door opened, I wheeled him into Dan's office, then went back to the waiting area and the white noise, paging through old issues of *Better Homes and Gardens* until the session was over.

Afterward, I helped Elias sit on the landing, facing forward this time, and bump down the stairs one at a time. Going down was much easier, we discovered. He got back into the wheelchair, with my assistance, and I rolled him to my waiting car.

Later I told myself, forcefully, that I could not be expected to be glad that my son had been in this accident. I could not be expected to accept his conclusion, on top of everything else I was expected to accept.

I told this to myself so vehemently it almost sounded like I was telling someone else, like God.

More than two years post-accident, Elias is himself full force: tough, funny, uncompromising. He lives alone, brooks no objection. We don't have daily interactions anymore—more like weekly ones. I have had to abandon the worries that used to keep me up at night, have had to ward off vivid fears: of fire, of burglars, of knives and guns, of hit-and-runs, of evil-intentioned strangers. Of another unexpected call, this time the death of me (him).

I think I have done well and deserve some recognition. My son thinks otherwise—or he doesn't think of me as a stand-up, an example. As someone to protect.

Maybe that's why today, as we are driving, talking as we often do about the arc of this strange experience, he again stops my heart with his casual observations.

I think I'm a different person since the accident, he begins.

I cringe because I think I know where this is going. Sensing my doubt, addressing it, he provides a few general examples: *Less arrogant, more grateful.*

Well, you don't know what would have happened without the accident, I say. *Probably you would have turned out the same.*

No, he responds quickly, with certainty. *No, I'm better. I've turned out better.*

Do you mean that you needed to change? And there wasn't any other way?

Now it's his turn to hesitate.

I've grown up, he says. *I'm less self-involved. Less. . . .* His voice trails off.

The question to end all questions hasn't been answered. I don't push it, though I want to stamp out this line of thinking, stop this smoldering mess before it spreads, engulfs both of us.

I am not as shocked as I was two years ago, however, when he suggested that this accident was somehow supposed to happen to him. Today, he's just pondering unforeseen benefits. I don't like the implications, though I understand his eagerness to express gratitude for his life, to find the positive in the aftermath.

But I am still surprised at the suggestion that this was our fate. I don't accept that verdict with the brightest face possible. He can't see my face, so he doesn't know that I grimace often, that my eyes cloud with mist; that I shake my head, sadly, almost unbidden.

It's the damn accompanying emotions that always stymie me. They lurk under my sunny surface, erupt in bouts of cursing:

Jesus.

Jesus Christ.

Jesus Christ Almighty.

Recently, I confessed to Elias that I swear more—too much—these days.

What do you say? he asked.

I told him and he laughed. *Mom, that's not swearing. If you're going to swear, make it count.*

I stay quiet in the car, listening. I can see he's also grappling with emotions, half-surprised at these insights that are just words—but words, words: all we have to invoke peace, to ward off fury and fear.

To pray if we choose.

WHEN IT HIT ME

For nearly three months, Elias lay in hospital beds—at Sanford Medical Center in Fargo, at Regency Hospital in Golden Valley, at Courage Center—and I arrived each morning to jumpstart his daily routine. I watched as he stood for the first time, as he marched in place, as he coaxed his sore muscles to complete the prescribed stretching routines with physical therapists.

When he returned home, I ferried him to multitudes of doctors' appointments: physical therapy, occupational therapy, hand and jaw therapy, psychotherapy. It was exhausting to account for the many ways in which the word *therapy* could be subdivided.

I stood silently while he boarded the small Metro Mobility van for the first time after it stopped at the end of our driveway on a dark September morning. That entire day—teaching my classes, grading in my office—I waited in my mind for his return.

I moved him—too soon, I thought—to his own apartment, listened to stories of his accomplishments: a spice rack assembled in woodshop, dinner cooked for guests in his own apartment, traveling by himself on a city bus to Southtown Mall, lunch at the taco truck with friends or at trusty Rudolph's Barbeque across the street from VLR.

That next summer, in 2016, I helped paint his newly purchased townhome, slathering color onto the scrubbed walls. I rubbed grease from kitchen countertops, vacuumed carpets until my arms would not stop vibrating. I drove to wherever and back—Lowe's, Home Depot, Menard's—to fetch what was missing: hardware, lightbulbs, screwdrivers, roller brushes, sponges, Lysol, gallons of paint. I went to various stores and bought sandwich meat, pop, bread, cookies.

At no time did I falter or collapse under the heavy reality of the situation.

Earlier today, I drove Elias to the Maple Grove transit station to catch a bus to Fargo. After much exploration, I found a parking spot on the third level of the garage. We exited the car; I walked him down to the lobby.

You can leave me here, he said. *There are always people around to help.*

Instead, I waited with him, though I know he's capable of taking care of himself. We munched our tasteless Burger King breakfast sandwiches, which we'd picked up along the way, as we sat on a bench in the industrial-looking waiting area.

Afterward, we walked outside to the makeshift bus stop, stood shivering in the half-mist of the late April morning, grass crisped by frost.

Elias was excited. He was traveling to attend in person a session of the education class he'd been taking via distance learning all semester. He would present his short teaching demonstration to his classmates, see friends, go to the gym, reconnect with his life before the accident.

When the bus pulled up, I relaxed my arm, and he relaxed his already light grip on my elbow.

Hey, bud, the bus driver said as he ambled over to greet us.

Obviously, Elias was the only passenger at this stop. Obviously, he was different, and I could tell that the driver had spotted that difference right away. He'd cast an overly casual glance in our direction, then averted his eyes toward the grass so as not to look directly at my son.

Then, trying to be helpful, the driver stepped forward, moving close to Elias. He presented an outstretched arm, seemingly proud of knowing what to do. But I watched him recalculate his role and reaction when Elias didn't immediately take his proffered arm.

Instead of reassessing his assumptions—realizing his error?—he turned to me and asked, *Is someone picking him up in Fargo?*

He spoke as if my son were not there, not a presence. What was he then? Apparently, someone the driver could not address directly.

Yes, several friends, Elias answered, confidently.

I nodded. Deliberately, I patted my son's fit arm, which still had a slight hold on my elbow.

See you on Saturday, I said, moving away, making sure that his fingers slid gently off.

I turned and started to walk away but was suddenly arrested by the sight of rows upon rows of parked cars: neat, sterile, inert.

Unsettled, I turned back, saw the driver pick up my son's bag, intending to carry it onto the bus. But Elias must have heard something: he reached out and took his bag from the driver. Guided by the sound of the engine, he walked on his own with his bag and his cane to the door of the bus, ascended the steps, turned the corner, disappeared behind the tinted windows.

Then, finally, I reacted. I thought, *This is* not *how it's supposed to be.*

My son doesn't need help transporting the bags he's already meticulously packed. He doesn't need an interpreter or a translator. He doesn't even need me to drive him around anymore. I offered; otherwise, he would have taken Metro Mobility to meet the bus. He would have faced this driver on his own.

I see now that this is how it's going to be. Everyone will assume the worst, will talk in loud, uninflected voices or ignore him altogether. Treat him like a child. Pet him, handle him with care. It's possible my presence makes this treatment more inevitable. I make him seem dependent.

I cried that day, finally, for the burden of misperception that will be added to his burden of navigating a world of darkness. In that parking garage, where the vista included yards of neatly parked Audis and Hondas, I dropped a few hot angry tears onto the pavement.

Then I went about my day.

What else should I have done?

SPATIAL

I recently discovered an enticing online IQ test while working in my campus office, so I began trying to assess my intelligence in the middle of a busy day, in between classes, hoping to squeeze into my full teaching schedule the potential affirmation that I'm actually smart.

I didn't really doubt my intelligence. However, once long ago, I took a supposedly accurate IQ test online, and my results came back with a score of zero. It was probably a mistake, but I moaned about it for weeks afterward. Perhaps because of that incident, I kept taking tests, hoping I could prove I'm smarter, in general, than I think.

This test was a standard spatial intelligence test, with every question formatted in the same way. Each presented a grid of nine boxes, three by three, like tic-tac-toe squares hemmed with borders. Inside each individual box was a shape, usually a variation of the shapes in the other boxes in the grid. There was always one blank box among the nine.

I understood what the test was asking me to do: to determine patterns (vertically and horizontally) and apply my knowledge to figure out what the shape in the blank box should be. I'd seen the same thing with numbers in sequence: discern the mathematical pattern, and you'll know the next number.

I never could parse numbers, but I thought I was doing splendidly with these shapes, humming along, mumbling out loud, describing to myself the pattern I was seeing in informal, nontechnical terms so that I could use it to predict what shape would belong in the empty space.

Starts with a shape, bisects it, then removes the original shape.

There are three of each shape: one's fully closed, one's open, then one has part of its head cut off.

I see one shape. Then its mirror image. Then the shapes combined.

Some of the problems were extremely complicated. I couldn't make out the pattern except to eliminate shapes that were already represented in the grid. In other words, sometimes I guessed.

After what must have been a long time, at least an hour, I realized that I had to go to class. Except that I hadn't finished the quiz. My results would be lost. If I wanted a score, and I did, I would have to start over later. Reluctantly, I left my office, but I kept the quiz open and active on my computer.

Because it was a nice day, and because I was teaching a poetry writing class, and because we'd just read a chapter about images, I was planning to send the students outside for twenty minutes to record what they were seeing, hearing, and smelling—a writing exercise focused on recording images of the world they lived in but often overlooked. I was hoping to sneak back to my office during that time and finish the test.

But as the students were filing out of the room, someone asked, *Can I leave my backpack here?*

Yes, I answered. I'd stay in the room. After all, some students hadn't arrived yet, and I didn't want them to see empty seats and assume that the class had been canceled.

I sighed heavily to myself, too dramatically.

It was only a stupid online test I was forfeiting—and my

results. But the shapes in their various twisted contortions were the only images I could picture as I sat preoccupied in my empty classroom. I was doing well on the test, I thought. I wanted to see if I was right.

Yes, I wanted to see that test: those dark shapes with their complex contours and the white space in between. I imagined rotating them in my mind to crack the code of the pattern. I struggled to hold their positions in my head, an abstract process that always challenges me.

Usually, all I could see clearly was my son, what the accident had done to him: his eyes cloudy, unable to note even pale light or dark or contrast (strands of gray in my auburn hair, for instance), the clothes his brothers wore, the label with dosage instructions on the bottle of ibuprofen.

He used to love tests like this; he was the best spatial thinker of my boys. That's why he was such a good marching band member. His mind could picture multiple rows and columns of marchers, along with their complicated movements and relationships; how the various steps and maneuvers would create visual patterns for the audience seated in bleachers above the field.

Now the manifestation of spatial in his life was not really spatial—that is, abstract. It was literal. Despite his spatial prowess, now that he can't see, he must physically feel the layout of any new room or environment by trailing his hand or cane around the full perimeter, noting and remembering the presence of furniture, doorjambs, countertops.

I have watched him perform this task. When he first moved into his townhome, for instance, he took himself on a guided tour, relying on his outstretched hands and cane to give him a template to commit to memory the spatial elements of each room: say, the number of steps between his bedroom door and the stairs to the main level.

All of us—his family—must remember, for our part, to preserve the known spatial dimensions of any given room, not to disrupt the spatial symmetry: to close the dishwasher, to push in chairs. We must not rearrange furniture or put things away in new places. We must also describe, out loud, his relation to physical objects so he can adjust and move independently.

Keep going, dude. There's a chair on your left and a table on your right.

Take two steps forward and then the card machine will be on your left. It's a chip reader.

He has spent a lot of his time with me, so sometimes my voice has been the only thing available to direct him. When I pick him up from someplace—the state fair, for instance, as I did a few days ago—all I must do to guide him is to open my mouth and speak.

On that day, spotting him in the distance, walking along the sidewalk near my car, I opened my window and cast my words into the air: *I'm right here.*

Immediately he pivoted, recognizing my voice. Then, following it, he extended his cane, sweeping it back and forth as he walked directly toward my vehicle, located the rear door, opened it, and got in—*cha-ching.*

The part I played was important; I provided spatial guidance by simply speaking. But I am certainly not perfect. Sometimes I stumble or mumble. Sometimes, in my commands, I sound spatially challenged, which I suppose I am.

Okay, come this way—I mean, turn to your right—left, I guess—sorry—and take a few steps.

I have long been known for mixing up my left and right, which is our joke, except that it is not a joke. I could make him run into doorjambs or poles or grocery-store displays or low-hanging tree limbs, or bump his knees on a chair, or even fall. In fact, except for making him fall, I have done all of these things. I didn't mean to misguide him, but I was still responsible for the outcomes, wasn't I?

When Elias first came home from the rehab center, a physical therapist advised me to remove all of the throw rugs from our house because they would present a tripping hazard.

He'll fall down the stairs, probably more than once, she warned. *Just be prepared.*

But in his inimitable way, my son has never experienced those challenges. He has yet to trip or stumble downstairs. He has navigated around an excitable dog and a family that frequently forgot to close the dishwasher. And I never removed those rugs.

Elias has excelled in his new spatial recognition of the world, as he has excelled in adjusting to all of his new challenges, even those he wasn't specifically prepared for. After the state fair pickup, when he had settled into the backseat, he erupted into a complaint, a rare occurrence for him. *I hate it when people talk about me. I know they're not trying to be offensive, but they are.*

I asked a series of probing questions, and the situation became clear. A couple of drunk young men had been trailing behind him, and he'd heard them talking. As their conversation revealed, they'd assumed that he was not only blind, but also deaf.

They had no notion of who he was and what he was capable of, so they spoke in normal tones, loud enough to penetrate the chaotic aural space of the fairgrounds, a space they had no idea he could expertly navigate.

Dude, look, there's Daredevil, one of them said.

I imagined, when I set aside my anger, that this young intoxicated man thought he was quite clever.

I wish they'd just talked to me, my son said, *and not about me.*

I made sympathetic comments in response to his story, wondering if they were helpful, if I were still capable of helping him. I said, *I'm sorry you had to hear that. It doesn't seem fair.*

Elias must face this reality. He's the same as he always has been, deep down, but he's different now on the surface. To realize that or to know him, people must engage in intimate face-to-face conversation, and relatively few will accept the challenge or invest the time.

That stupid spatial intelligence test I'd started in my campus office had nothing to do with our current situation. On one level, I wasn't thinking of my son when I clicked on the link. On another level, it had everything to do with it. From here on, everything would remind me of him. He was always in my thoughts, whether I acknowledged this or not.

I have resumed a daily life that is so close to my former life as to be indistinguishable. Yet my former life is gone. Few people can see that from the outside. Sometimes I close my eyes at night when I get up to use the bathroom or go downstairs if I can't sleep—a futile gesture, but I do it anyway.

Recently, Elias traveled to Fargo to rehearse with the NDSU marching band, for which he is a staff member. He had written the drum parts for this season's show. He had traveled alone, stayed in a hotel room with a kitchen, where he had cooked his own meals. None of that was a highlight for him.

The highlight of the trip was that several section leaders had challenged him to a march-off. Who could best march in a straight line, performing in the precise, measured way that marching band requires? The challenge was that section leaders would don blindfolds and Elias would simply march on his own.

It wasn't even a contest. The section leaders couldn't manage even a straight line. They veered to the right or the left, took uneven steps, while Elias, blind to everything but his internal sense of space, marched straight ahead, taking steps of uniform length.

Then they compared turns. Elias was already the winner, but he demonstrated his superior skills anyway: he pivoted, executing a perfect ninety-degree-angle turn on cue. Just like the old days. He'd always been an excellent marcher, carrying inside him some grid that he could easily mimic on the field. That sight was always there. It's still there, housed internally, where he can access it.

Sight is both literal and abstract. So is space.

I wish my son had his literal sight.

I wish I could adjust as well as he has.

LIGHT

The edges of clouds are on fire, singed by the setting sun. I have my own fire, too, in my small steel firepit, a self-contained bowl, burning the season's first dry brush and twigs, torn from our trees during winter's fury. I am sitting on my backyard patio, enjoying the first really fine night of spring, holding my hands out to the fire's heat, and looking up as small balloons of ash float toward the sky.

The blue of the sky is an illusion, a false ceiling. It looks like the lid of the world, but it is really a door to the infinite, a sign that there is no lid or cover at all. I don't want to consider infinity—endlessness—when I gaze upward for signs of peace or weather. It's a good thing I can see something that looks like a boundary.

Even though it is not a boundary, but a portal to the endlessness that is space, I am comforted.

Why is the sky blue? The NASA website tells me it's because light energy from the sun travels toward earth in waves, short and long, in all the colors of the rainbow. But blue light waves are short, so they are more prone to scattering as they encounter the air of the earth's atmosphere in their travels.[7]

That makes sense, doesn't it? That scattering—that chaos—makes the sky look blue, though both sky and blue are substitutes, simple approximations of complex concepts.

I personally resist scattering. I like to keep my ideas in my own head, where they are safe. If I sent them outward, they would take some of me—some atoms of thought, some element of my conviction flaking off my physical body. I need that body to remain intact, at the molecular and all other levels.

Sight is how we navigate the world we have been given. We value it above other senses. Because we can see, we think we can see clearly. Microscopic creatures notwithstanding, we believe in our own vision. *I saw it with my own eyes,* we say. But we can only see a specified distance. Anything beyond our sight is literally out of sight. This fact takes on a poignant truth for babies, who believe their parents disappear when they leave the room. Parents only exist when they can be seen.

As we grow, we come to understand that sight isn't needed to confirm reality. Photos will do, or first-hand accounts, or imagination. Space, for instance: the planets, whatever is there when we look up—it's real, it's there, even if we can't clearly see it. It's so vast that it's not even measured in fathomable terms. Space. com confirms that the universe is approximately 13.8 billion years old. The distance between earth and the edge of the observable universe is 46 billion light years.[8]

Every time I drive Elias somewhere, the trip should be mundane, but it's not. Conversation elevates our travels; we have only words to light up our worlds. We count on them to help us see beyond ourselves.

Recently, I dropped him off at a haircut appointment. On the way, he accused me of not remembering where the salon was. I accused him of not trusting my judgment. So far, we were in familiar territory.

But then our conversation took a sudden turn. We were parking (proof that I did remember where the salon was) when he said, seemingly out of the blue, *I wonder what my life would have been like if I had been in the accident but not lost my sight?*

We got out of the car. I walked to his side, and, as usual, he gripped my right elbow lightly but firmly while wielding his cane in his other hand. We progressed toward the entrance, talking about his question as we walked.

He would have graduated sooner from college with less stress, we began. Bought a bigger house, probably. Been a rock star by now, complete with a teaching job and a sports car.

It would have been so easy, he said.

I nodded in agreement, which he did not see.

We know our reality. We know what a blessed existence we both live. Still.

It's weird, he said. *I don't even know what I look like.*

I heard his words as I hauled the salon door open, guided him verbally inside.

Do I even look the same?

You look the same, basically, I confirmed, *except your left eye is a little funky. And you have that scar on the left side of your face—remember? It cuts into your mustache.*

You know what's even weirder? he continued. *I don't know what you look like. I haven't seen you in three years.*

I nearly froze in place but managed to steady myself and guide him to his hairdresser's cubicle. Then, because someone else was picking him up, I left him in her capable hands and reversed course to my car.

On the drive home, I was acutely aware of details: recently

painted lines on the road, dead raccoon at the road's edge, Arby's sign flashing in my rearview mirror.

Once I arrived, I saw the sunset showing off as usual: pinks and oranges splashed across the sky. But the colors, I knew, were a false promise. The sky does not really change color; clouds are merely reflecting light, not embodying it. The sky itself is not even tangible space. We recite its known size, but we don't have the capacity to visualize how large it is.

Sitting quietly at home did not quiet my head. Never had the truth been so stark: *I haven't seen you in three years*. Of course.

Here I had been ferrying him to appointments, hovering in the background, believing that he was imagining walking beside me—the physical me.

When I think of myself in the world, I think of how I look: shape, substance. Heft. I had assumed that's what he was thinking—imagining—as well.

This truth he'd uttered was a scorching one, even if he'd uttered it innocently. It removed the lid from my conception of us—his trustful following, my confident leading. Somehow his trust was like vision. He could see me through my actions—the actual me.

I have taken on the dimensions of a concept. I exist without being seen—as a voice, the only observable part of me.

All of his world is conceptual now. The literal edges have vanished, except what he can feel by touching boundaries—walls, counters, doorways, my elbow. If he had to live outside, nomadic, the world would be his sky: endless, illimitable, unfathomable. But there.

All evening, as light faded and the infinite sky dissolved into darkness, I walked around my house: heavy, slow, ponderous. I had no thoughts. They had disappeared into the infinite recesses of my brain. I simply plodded, up and down stairs, bearing this new idea, testing its weight.

My son lives in total darkness, in an immeasurable world.

Beside him, my voice makes me real, makes the world real, supplies assurance that he can move forward without disaster.

I imagine all of the light in the world in my throat, refracted and scattering—so words can be formed out of the void.

GOD SAID

The focus of Elias's recovery was never mainly spiritual. Though the accident raised obvious questions about faith, God, agency, and fate; though we all used the word *miracle* often in the first few weeks; though Elias himself confessed to me several months after the accident that he was willing to consider the existence of God because he shouldn't have survived, it was never the primary lens through which he or I viewed the unfolding events.

It *was* the primary lens for others, however—Rich and Kay, for instance—along with relatives and friends who'd left messages on the CaringBridge site.

But since then, as I have reflected, I have been reminded that much of my life has been a spiritual journey—a struggle, more accurately—and that despite my withdrawal from organized religion some years ago, I still haven't rejected belief entirely. I believe in *something*, though I can't define it exactly. That makes me a bit like Melville, who couldn't comfortably believe or disbelieve in his later life.

The tug and pull of the spiritual for these past five years, as I see it now, is just one individual cog in the wheel of my own long journey toward—well, perhaps it is better not to name the destination, since I am clearly still seeking.

September 1990. Was it dread or curiosity?

I stood in front of my folding chair, one of many in a neat row. My head was bowed, my hands clasped. I was trying not to look around—that would be unseemly—at the bodies suddenly buckling, falling to the floor. Someone usually appeared to catch them, ease their way down. Would I be next?

The room was hushed, filled with whispers: those hardly-words gathered, carpeting the silence. I waited in pure antici-pation. I didn't need to hear any word; most of them would be unintelligible anyway—people were speaking in Tongues.

I was attending a weekend conference devoted to the Holy Spirit, that third member of the Trinity, the most mysterious and evasive. So far It/He had successfully evaded me, or vice versa. While fellow congregants were keeling over left and right—*slain in the Spirit*—I remained upright. Some hidden sin or doubt, I was sure, kept me from experiencing what had become expected that weekend.

The conference had begun innocently enough, with the head pastor assuring all of us who were gathered that the spirit works in many ways. He himself was not a "touchy-feely" person, he said. He didn't expect to swoon.

But soon swooning was in, and even the pastor went down while I remained upright, practically begging for a sign. I wanted—needed—to demonstrate that my faith was authentic. Everyone else in attendance seemed assured. I worked so hard to be open to the experience that my stomach knotted and my lower back began to ache.

Focus, I told myself, assuming what I thought was an open, inviting posture. Curiosity did turn to dread then. Maybe I was not a true believer, and soon someone was going to find that out.

Late during the second night, I walked alone to the end of a dock on the property, took off my shoes and socks, and dangled my feet in the lake water. The moon was high in the sky, painting a luminous streak across the surface of the lake, creating a swath of light so beautiful it beckoned me to dive in and become part of it.

The day's events, which had been spooling endlessly in my mind, stopped replaying. I sat without thoughts, at peace, kicking slowly in a lazy rhythm.

Nothing happened to me that weekend—nothing physical, demonstrable—though I wanted the white-hot presence to overtake me. It occurred to me I could fake it. Who would ever know?

Some of the swooners might be faking it. That thought, though it arrived unbidden, proved my weakness: my faith was in jeopardy.

Within a week of arriving home, what I had just begun in a gray corner of my mind to suspect was confirmed: pregnant again. That would help explain the sudden craving for a Snickers on the drive up, maybe the otherworldly peace on the dock. Hormones.

This third child would cement the cracked and crumbling foundation of a troubled marriage for a few years. He would also add a light to our lives that would persist beyond all expectation.

We named him Elias, which means *Jehovah is God.*

When I was growing up, my favorite memory of church was the scent of incense: mysterious, delectably spicy, hints of warm cinnamon and cloves.

On Good Friday, incense made the prayers more real: Jesus must rise from the dead when the room we'd prepared for his return smelled so good.

When I kissed his plaster feet in front of the congregation—a gesture I despised—I pretended to be overcome. *If that's what it takes to get him here, to notice me,* I thought, *I'll do it.*

Beads press my palms. Mary presses them, imparting her gift.

Pray the rosary, she advises. If I can pray it with her, that will be great.

I'm never closer to God than when I'm praying like this, she says.

We are students at St. Thomas, a private Catholic college. We are also friends who have gone on several weekend retreats together. She knows I am seeking a deeper faith, a firmer connection with God.

Once I see what's involved, though, I don't even try: rote prayers are distasteful to me. They are precisely what I'm trying to move beyond. But I know she's trying to help me.

This decade is Our Father and this one is Hail Mary, I hear her say.

I wonder to myself, *Do I pray out loud? Do I kneel? Can I add my own words? What if I get bored? What if I fall asleep?*

What's a decade?

She doesn't offer any explanation. How easy it would be to press her, or look up the information, or ask one of my professors. (I'm enrolled in a theology class, for Christ's sake.)

I note the repetition and smirk at the implied message: *God will listen only if I am insistent in the most mindless way.* Out of goodness, I hope, I listen to Mary but remain noncommittal. She is trying to help me. But I don't want this kind of help.

I must not be a good Catholic.

When she leaves, I stash her gift—the beads—in a drawer, where they coil blackly, rattle like a snake every time I open and close it.

As Elias and I turn a corner in a Hy-Vee grocery store, a woman bears down on us suddenly, her hand already extended, before we are even close enough to touch.

Hi, I'm M__, she says.

We shake hands; then she turns to Elias.

You're blind?

Yes.

What happened?

He explains briefly: the accident, his recovery. Three years past the trauma, he is able to speak about it in a matter-of-fact way.

You have a positive attitude. I know God led me to you tonight. Can I pray for you?

Yes, he says.

My son has coached me to let him speak for himself in public. Something doesn't seem right about this encounter, but I hold my tongue.

Suspicious, I grip the handle of the shopping cart.

I'm going to put my hand on your shoulder, this woman says.

She's going to pray now, I realize. I can't look at Elias, nor up, nor down, my learned posture of submission. I look instead toward the pharmacy section on my left.

She launches into a passionate plea: *Father God, bind up the cause of this blindness. I claim this healing in your son's name, I lay it at the feet of your son, Jesus.*

I recognize her vocabulary and fervent insistence from an earlier faith I'd never had the courage to adopt wholly—or wholly reject. I keep my eyes wide open, unable to close them to this scene. We are in the middle of the health and beauty section, surrounded by pleasantly colored bottles of liquid, pleasant but muted scents. Eventually, I do close my eyes. It's less embarrassing not to see who's staring. But my gesture makes me complicit.

She pauses after a minute's worth of pleading.

Can you see now? she asks.

Until this moment, I have not realized her full intent.

When he shakes his head, she continues, *I'm going to try again.*

I close my eyes more tightly now, and my hands squeeze the cart handle until my knuckles begin to ache. I can't see whether she still has a hand on his shoulder. But I hear her language ramp up.

After her second attempt, I worry. How many times will she pray? Will she *pray without ceasing?*

My own doubts surface: *I'm the one preventing this miracle from happening.*

But someone must intervene.

She is intervening (she thinks).

Her fourth attempt ends. I open my eyes, finally, and see her pull herself up, adjust.

I'll keep praying for you, she says, guiding her cart away.

We—my son and I—stand silent a moment, then move toward an aisle we haven't visited yet, where we choose the last grocery items he needs. Rounding another corner, I see the woman, bent over the handle of her cart, texting furiously on her phone.

Elias and I save our critical conversation for later. When later comes, my son does himself proud: he has learned to see the humor in it.

She was the one who looked ridiculous, he says. *Not me.*

It all had to start somewhere.

My adolescent rebellion was typical: I tried cigarettes (once), pot (more than once), and alcohol (many times). I was smart, I was arrogant—measurable progress of my rebellion. But my grades never suffered. I was an excellent student. I thought I could pull it off: be both studious and a partier. I mostly did pull it off.

Somewhere in the middle of my charade, a friend invited me to attend a weekend retreat. I agreed because it would satisfy a requirement for my quickly-approaching Confirmation. However, I was determined that no religious experience would change me: I would attend only to cross something off a list.

But something happened to me that weekend. God got to me.

When I returned home, my former life was over. I quit drinking and getting high; I was convinced that they were wrong. I didn't understand either what had happened or my response to it, yet it had gotten me what I wanted: attention. Obedience to this godly authority had made me feel loved and useful, part of a community.

Ironically, my new burst of faith also gave me the boldness to institute a new rebellion. During Mass at the Catholic church our family attended, during the Prayer over the Gifts, the priest would say, *Pray, brothers and sisters, that our sacrifice may be acceptable to God the Almighty Father.*

And the congregation would reply, *May the Lord accept the sacrifice at your hands, for the praise and glory of His name, for our good, and the good of all His Church.*

Every Sunday, dutifully—under my breath—I changed the words: *for our good, and the good of all his churches.*

Plural. And lower case.

Probably, this made no difference. But I stood proudly next to my mother, the staunchest Catholic I knew, quietly mouthing my sacrilege.

Long ago I decided that there is no devil, no potent force intervening to keep me from God. Partly I learned that from books. Partly I learned it from experience. There is only a broken world, broken people in it, trying to find. . . .

How do I know what people are seeking?

Driving home from a poetry reading, I think about what I will write tonight. Then I see the sign in front of the First Baptist Church near my house. It says, *Jesus Satisfies.*

The sign catches me off guard. I laugh to myself in the dark interior of my car.

It's the word *satisfies* that tickles me. So decidedly sexual.

Many years ago, newly separated from my husband—lonely, doubtful, trying to decide what to do about my marriage and my questions about faith—I tried some new spiritual practices that convinced me I still had belief, even if I believed differently from the Baptists with whom I had gone to church for some eight years.

I got into the habit of meditating before sleep. I was still getting used to living alone with my three sons. When I finished meditating, I prayed directly in the old way, adding a few simple words: *Please be with me—sleep with me—tonight.* It was hokey and juvenile, but it was also practical.

I was scared out of my wits. I desired protection mostly from my imagination, which conjured intrusions: burglars, rapists, desperate drug addicts. We did live on the north side of Minneapolis; crime was not unheard of. The corner store, Carlson Drug, was robbed once or twice a year.

A grad student at the time, I also had the mystic Margery Kempe on my mind, her flagrant love talk about Jesus, whom she considered to be her actual husband. She refused to have sex with her earthly husband on His account.

One night after prayer, as I was relaxing into my night posture, my body lit up unexpectedly, all along the length of it. I lay in my double bed, that so recently had held a husband, and felt tingling sensations: electric, provocative, and—yes—sexual.

I can't explain it. But I remember it with longing.

In the movie *Shadowlands,* the character of C. S. Lewis says, "Prayer doesn't change God—it changes me." His wife had terminal cancer. He was not praying for the miracle of her healing, but for the ability to live through and beyond her death—to want to keep going in spite of the loss.

I connect this scene with all of the wordless prayers I have flung to the sky when my children have been in trouble because of drugs or totaled cars or because they have snuck out their bedroom windows or been caught shoplifting, or when Elias was hanging onto life, barely, the only sign of his earthly presence a chest that rose and fell, the sound of a machine breathing for him.

The writings of C. S. Lewis single-handedly taught me longing, the *Chronicles of Narnia* especially. But since reading them as a twelve-year-old, I have associated the keenest desires with frustration. Aslan does not always appear when summoned—in fact, he hardly ever does. No one can command him, even his Chosen.

Even Lucy was limited in her visits to Narnia. Ultimately, Aslan kept her from himself, the thing she wanted most.

Recently, I tried to reinsert some meditative breathing exercises into my routine. I figured they wouldn't hurt, maybe even help me process the grief and anger about the accident that I was keeping hidden, mostly. I experienced these feelings as a profound agitation, an intense focus on work and other necessary tasks that kept me from reflecting. My spirit had become unsettled. I had been sinking into myself in inverse proportion to Elias's progress. I had become awash in a wave of silent rage and worry.

The centering prayer I was going to try again was modeled after the practices of Saint Ignatius Loyola. Long ago, he had proposed a simple concept: breathe in deeply; then, on the exhale, focus on the solar plexus, the entrance to the soul, as he believed. Envision going as deep as possible, diving into the interiority where the spirit (of God, maybe) lives.

The friend who introduced me to this practice many years ago counseled me not to expect instant results. This kind of breathing exercise was a practice, a discipline. I would feel a surer connection with God over time, but not in a week. It was harder than it seemed, she also advised. Breathing like this, sinking into the center of my own body, fending off distractions, was a spiritual challenge. Years ago, I kept it up (religiously, as they say), and I did actually feel better over time. More peaceful. More like myself.

My first few recent sessions at night, after that long interval, seemed to go well. I sensed a familiar sensation just at the juncture of the two halves of my ribcage. Now all I had to do was continue, and I would know the presence of the universe (the word I substitute for God when I don't want to admit I miss prayer) and be comforted by it. Maybe I would even begin to feel as hopeful as my son felt.

But on the next few nights when I tried to implement the breathing, I was distracted; I couldn't do it. My mind was filled with details of the list I was composing mentally for the next day—what I thought I needed to accomplish. Song lyrics leaped into my mind, unbidden, in snatches, never a whole verse. Though I concentrated so hard that I could feel my body tense, there was nothing but a dull sensation in my belly.

After several nights of this frustration, I decided to place my open palm on the place where my concentration gathered. Maybe the slight warmth of my hand would help me focus, help direct the deepening sensation I sought.

When I placed my hand there, on the location of my concentration, I discovered I was way off. My hand lay several inches below my solar plexus. I had lost my bearings, it seemed; I didn't even know my own body.

I was failing at meditation.

In the dark, I opened my eyes, which had remained closed because I equated that with reverence. I saw the faint blue light of the digital clock to my left. I saw the pale glow of the streetlight on the ceiling as it slanted in and was deflected upward through the blinds. I looked up to where light's presence was peripheral, at the edges.

I saw light—tangible light—and felt no peace.

When I'm hiking at St. Croix State Park or Frontenac or Banning or Nerstrand Big Woods or Wild River—all of the places where I encounter myself and the created world—I pray the trails are deserted. They are my chapel. I hike hard, reciting poems I have committed to memory: William Wordsworth's, Mary Oliver's, Chaucer's General Prologue to *The Canterbury Tales*:

> WHAN that Aprille with his shoures soote
> The droghte of Marche hath perced to the roote[9]

Pierced to the root, the text says. Yes, nature does prick us in the heart. The words remind me that, if this is all there is, the tactile world, then I've been given a lot. As I walk, I finger variegated leaves of trillium and pop plump thimbleberries into my mouth. When I spy tree branches that have fallen in a dense grove, I see that they are caught and suspended by other branches. Oak cradles birch; basswood's smooth youthful branch lies in the crooked arms of elm.

There is a pulse here, a heartbeat I match with my stride. The poems I recite are prayers, are gratitude—for existence, however fleeting—for the sight of raspberry canes intertwined with ferns and grasses, all of the shoots rising.

Having abandoned much doctrinal certainty, I am banking on this kind of relating. I touch the infinite in the woods—beauty that perseveres even in death, in dying.

When Nicodemus doesn't understand spirit, Jesus scolds him.

I pull weeds that thrive in spring: those shaped like small fronds of lettuce, the ones that resemble pea plants, the ones I dub *crazy grass.* To tend requires selection. I prune and prune and water. One must do this on one's knees, exhaling into soil and breathing in the scent of cut grass and lilacs.

Elias will never see me again. This changes nothing about how we interact, except when it does. Hugs are sometimes awkward; our bodies must work to find the right posture. But we connect— with words or silence—or we laugh at some stupid joke, or he pokes fun at me, a gesture so commonplace it floods my senses.

When the sky darkens or brightens or the sun sets or there's a rainbow or my green beans are ready to harvest or someone pulls out in front of me on the highway, I tell him what I see, and we talk.

WHAT END THERE CAN BE

I have just found out that Elias is moving to Fargo. He says he needs to get on with his life. Though I am familiar with the general sentiment behind that statement, I am surprised to hear it from him. He has seemed, always, to defy clichés, but now he is about to live one. In addition, there's a girl involved (no kidding).

I have arranged for a moving truck (against the objections of my mother heart) because he has, characteristically, not taken care of the details himself. In addition, I will help him pack and move. On short notice. With the expectation that I will bring boxes and packing material.

I have borne it, birthed it, made it come to pass—what he wants.

Last week, toiling in my office at the end of a long day, I heard the fire alarm go off. There had been an earlier email announcing a drill, but I had forgotten that warning.

I closed my office door, ignored the warning, and resumed my nearly finished work: preparation for that night's community ed memoir class. Minutes later I stuffed papers and folders into my bag, opened my door, exited into the hallway, where the obnoxious tolls of the fire alarm were still pulsing.

I should have been ashamed. I had disregarded the alarm, whose purpose was to protect me, teach me what to do in a real emergency. But I was irritated. The loud noise of the alarm beat time in my ears; I felt the shock of the decibels in my body. The building shook with the pulsing noise, and flashing lights mounted in hallway corners provided visual accompaniment as I made my way to the nearest exit.

Once outside, my irritation only increased. Crowds of people strolled slowly toward the parking lot, blocking my way. I wove around them, snorting. I kept my head down to hide my exasperation and something underneath it: a purposeful outside coupled with a seething inside. It was not part of my plan to fall prey to the casual conversations of students on their phones, crowing about a ten-minute break from class or complaining about their lovers in public.

Echoing in my body, almost like a faint siren itself, was this realization: I was always in a hurry these days, impatient and enraged when something altered my plan. More than that, I strained forward every day, dogged by some gnawing pressure, dragging behind me a cartful of tasks that were my responsibility. Even a short list felt like too much—a heaviness to haul around.

It was an achy feeling. I ached, also, to get out from under it—to stand peacefully, unburdened.

In late September, the air was still warm and a bit damp. The day was sunny, with clouds like delicate spiderwebs stretched across the sky. Yet this weighty urgency pressed down on my shoulders.

I could have stopped and faced myself. Instead, I went home, fixed dinner, reviewed notes before leaving for the class I knew would go well because I was prepared.

In my therapist's office, one throw pillow rests behind my back and another—the one with fringes that I mess and straighten as we talk—sits on my lap.

I have given her my check-in number for the day. (*On a scale of one to ten, how am I feeling? Seven.*) She asks me what is behind that innocent number.

Elias is moving—soon, I begin.

I list my frustrations relating to this fact: *He hasn't planned carefully enough, doesn't have a job, is rushing it.*

Yes, I have shared these concerns with him—for we are honest with each other.

This move forces me to face . . . well, the accident—all of it.

I start to tear up, so I reach for a tissue.

I have not come to terms with it, I say, struggling to keep my voice even. *I'm not sure I ever will. Does that sound too dramatic?*

The tissue absorbs tears before they run down my cheeks. Even as my mouth works to explain, my voice wavers, but I get it under control through a measured exhalation of words.

I may want to fall apart—I lean in that direction, toward surrendering to my emotions; but in the end I can't, not even with a therapist.

Late in the first summer after the accident, after Elias had already been home for several months, Tim and I tried to do activities that seemed normal. The vehicle of our lives had been sideswiped, but the car still ran—right?

My sister invited us to a Twins baseball game, courtesy of her financial planner, who pays for a suite at the stadium. We ate free food, drank free wine, sat in hard plastic seats, and occasionally watched the game.

My out-of-town niece was there, whom I hadn't seen since the weekend we'd found out that Elias was blind, almost five months earlier. She asked how I was doing—*really.*

I drink more than I probably should, I said, lifting the glass of wine I held casually in my hand. She held one, too, and we touched glasses—equal.

Of course! How could you not? she said.

Sometimes I wonder if I will suddenly fall apart in public, I told her.

She looked at me keenly, with concern. *I wonder what that would look like,* she murmured.

I don't know. Maybe scream a lot? Maybe say something inappropriate? Maybe. . . .

I couldn't envision it, so it could never be.

I want to keep my children safe. I must. Isn't that every parent's goal?

From their earliest childhoods, my most pressing fear was that someday I wouldn't be able to protect them. My phobia in those days was specific: our car plunging off a bridge into the swirling river below. Thoughts of losing control in this way invaded my dreams, my downtime before sleep. Those frightening fantasies forced me to plan. I would have to get everyone out of their car seats, out through windows or doors, somehow, before releasing them, my small handful of minnows, to swim by themselves or cling to my body so we might rise to the surface together.

If you look at the word *blind* long enough, it doesn't look like a real word. Still, we have many clichés about blindness in our lexicon:

Blind as a bat
Blind drunk
The blind leading the blind
A blind alley
Love is blind
They robbed you blind
Blind luck
Turn a blind eye

A blind date

We use these phrases casually, without comprehending the magnitude.

Elias is always a blind date (ha ha). If he drinks too much, he's going to be blind drunk—both funny and serious.

If the room spins and he can't see it. . . .

He turns his blind eyes everywhere. That's how he interacts with the world.

Tim and I have traveled to northern California several times, and Mono Lake is a favorite stop. It is surrounded by an area of volcanic craters, young ones, that last erupted seven hundred years ago. I have walked the rim of an inactive one there, have gathered obsidian and pumice in my hands, stones that broadcast the story of the area's history, the omnipresent potential disaster.

I have not ever been afraid during any of those visits; the word *volcano* hasn't fully registered. All seems calm, though my feet literally navigate a disrupted, uneven bed of stones. I wobble over them, never solidly placed. Evidence presents itself, yet eruptions seem remote to me, impossible. Because the surface seems stable, I cannot imagine the interior or the potential that it will erupt in deadly, flowing lava.

What makes us count on a safe life? Maybe lawsuits and legal battles, which suggest that harm is an anomaly, completely avoidable—its presence detestable, shocking, grounds for lawsuits. But some of these lawsuits are frivolous, inadequate. They make us believe safety is a right.

The agent of my son's blindness took away any certainty I may have once had that safety is a guarantee. It aches to think so, but it is true.

I also ache to recall a story that a Mother's against Drunk Driving advocate told me when Elias was still at Regency. She was trying to prepare me for our upcoming court dates. Laws and transactions of justice are inadequate, she said. She related the story of a recent drunk-driving crash in which the passenger, a woman, had died, while the driver, the drunk and high boyfriend, had lived.

Because the victim had died, she remained at the mercy (even in death) of her addicted boyfriend, who testified that she had gone crazy. He said that she had hit him and distracted him as he was driving (drunk), which had caused him to swerve off the road and crash.

It was her fault, he insisted.

The jury bought it: he suffered no penalty.

This could happen to you, the advocate said as I sat in my vinyl hospital chair, stiffly upright and listening.

I know it is a lie that I can control other people's actions. Yet I ache to keep my children safe. And I can't—I haven't.

Control, yes—the double-edged sword. The accelerator and brakes of our existence.

Elias's girlfriend, Kaity, who will help him transition to Fargo and a life away from his family—of course, I mean me—has an adopted younger brother Kash, the son of a heroin-addicted relative. Her parents adopted him just as they were about to become empty nesters. He was eight months old at the time.

Kash is an anomaly, a survivor. He is profoundly deaf in one ear. He is legally blind, but he can see some things, up close, though that may change over time. His cognitive capacity is limited. Most seriously, he has a nervous-system disorder that prevents him from feeling pain. He could cut himself, fall downstairs, get burned, and this would not register as pain for him nor tell him that he should stop what he is doing.

Given this condition, other family members must be his eyes and safety (though he is living proof that safety is a myth, his mother's agency having determined his condition). It is difficult to imagine others living with this condition, to visualize how vigilant a life his family must lead.

I have pictures on my phone that Elias sent to me, of him and Kash. Elias had been visiting his girlfriend's family on a hot summer afternoon, and they had all gone to cool off in the above-ground pool in the backyard. In the pictures, Elias is standing in waist-deep water, holding Kash, now about four years old: holding him at arm's length in one shot, lifting him high in the air in the other.

In both photos, Elias is smiling joyfully—a laughing smile—and Kash, though his face is only partially visible, is also grinning. These two, who can barely or not at all see each other, are having a grand time together.

These are images I will keep, images that Elias keeps in his mind.

That kid is so great, he told me.

Composure: my beloved forced steadiness. It enabled me to ask rational questions of doctors, advocate for Elias when he was in the hospital. It helped me insist that he got what he needed: X rays, water on a sponge, extra blankets, sedatives, explanations. It enabled me to return to my full-time teaching job, to plan the rest of my career, to set goals, to appreciate the gift of a stable job.

The accident and its aftermath have threatened my composure, but they have also preserved it. I wear, still, a protective coating that stabilizes my thoughts and the emotions they engender. They can bubble away, but they will never erupt.

I have had to undergo a slow awakening, against the mettle of will and want; have had to lift my head from the pillow of its own disconsolation; have had to learn to say *yes, yes*—not to the world as remembered, but as reimagined.

Before I left Elias in Fargo for good, I got to meet his girlfriend's family, including Kash, in person for the first time. As we entered the house, Kash, arms flung out, fingers wiggling in excitement, ran over. *E! E! E! E!* he squealed.

He's been waiting for you all day, said his mother to my son. Turning to me, she said, by way of introduction, *Elias is Kash's favorite.*

Elias picked Kash up and held him on his lap during most of my visit.

After a couple of hours spent eating and talking, I drove away. Alone, I cried in earnest. I have ferried my son into the next stage of his life. This new family will take over from here, will see him more than I will, because they live only an hour east of Fargo, while we live almost four hours away.

I missed him already as I made my way home, but when I stopped for gas and texted that message to him, he didn't respond.

I thought he would always live close by, that I could tend his life, help him grow and thrive and aim for the future he wants.

It is bitter and it is sweet—because that is what I have done.

The thing is: Elias would love Kash, even if he could see him.

The thing is: even as a baby, Elias was set apart. A few days after we came home from the hospital, I was nursing him when he unlatched and turned his head suddenly in the direction of his brothers, who were laughing together in the next room.

His action took me by surprise. I thought, *He has heard them speak and recognizes their voices.*

More profoundly: *He knows them.*

I sat on the couch, waiting for him to return to his hunger, milk soaking my shirt. I thought, *What kind of sensitive child have I brought into the world?*

The roads I travel in my daily rounds are roads I have traveled often with Elias during the past four years. I hauled him, laden with drumsticks, backpack, and water bottles, to marching band rehearsal. I drove him to doctors' appointments, to Hy-Vee, to the post office, to FedEx for work. I deposited him on many doorsteps. These routes, crisscrossing our geographic area, tracked our progress, made a shape.

We etched a series of paths I see now—*feel*—as I drive alone:

The exit I missed one time, on the way to Maple Grove High School, that caused us to drive almost ten miles out of the way before I could turn around, retrace my route. Elias remained patient, though it was likely I would get him to rehearsal late.

The road that curves past Mercy Hospital, where I took him, one misty night, when he developed a sudden tremendous headache that turned out to be the beginning of cellulitis, which landed him in the hospital on the second anniversary of the accident (the night I thought fate might be a real concept).

The long stretch of interstate on the way to Fargo, during which he played the *Hamilton* soundtrack for me for the first time; during which I always fear envisioning the accident and feel glad that I still can't make myself envision it.

The stoplight by his townhome, where he lived for three years, where I often turned the wrong way and consequently suffered his good-natured ribbing.

The crowded parking lots of all the restaurants we frequented for lunch because we spent so much time together: Noodles, Rose Garden, Panera.

In the car, we were always in conversation. I kept my eyes on the road but aimed my voice in his direction, wanting to drive and listen well—do all things well for his sake—focus on all of our destinations: errands, health, acceptance.

The silence of the car now agitates me. Now it's just me and my errant thoughts.

I continue to traverse the land where Elias learned his freedom, the land that launched him into a new orbit—*solo*, we might say, applauding.

It is the land where I live, where I must keep learning what freedom entails: for him, exhilaration; for me, longing, which is an essential part of love.

AFTERWORD

In November 2022, Elias and Kaity, the one who captured his heart and his imagination, got married in Fargo. Their wedding was a testament to their partnership, which is as respectful and equal as any I have seen. They built their wedding arch together, out of books they got free from a secondhand store. They had a voicemail guestbook so that Elias could hear the guests' messages and not have them read to him. They included a hand-fasting ceremony so that the knot they created could be a tactile reminder for Elias of their union and partnership. In their first dance as a married couple, they swayed slowly at first with the music. Then suddenly the beat changed, and they were swing-dancing, whirling around the parquet dance floor, a routine they had clearly rehearsed.

Elias spends his time working for the NDSU marching band, writing drum parts and rehearsing the percussion section. He occasionally gives private drum lessons. He sings with a local barbershop chorus. He has set up a workshop in his garage, where he practices his craft of woodworking. He has built, so far, a large bar for his sister-in-law's wedding, a bench for their table, several birdhouses, and a cutting board for me. He's working on a coffee table now. True to his own vision of the world, he told me, when I expressed some concern for his safety, *The only time I even came close to injuring myself, it was my fault—and I only needed a few stitches. I was in a hurry, and I thought: I'm just making one small cut. I don't need the safety guide.*

He and Kaity have two cats and a tortoise. Both cats love him. He is still Kash's favorite.

NOTES

1. Michael Pollan, *Omnivore's Dilemma: A Natural History of Four Meals* (New York: Penguin, 2006), 349.

2. Thomas Hardy, "The Convergence of the Twain," in *The Norton Anthology of English Literature*, ed. M. H. Abrams (New York: Norton, 1975), 2287–88.

3. Robert Frost, "Out, Out—," in *The Poetry of Robert Frost*, ed. Edward Connery Lathem (New York: Holt, 1969), 136–37.

4. Milk Carton Kids, "Hope of a Lifetime," *The Ash & Clay* (Los Angeles: Anti Records, 2013), compact disc.

5. Milk Carton Kids, "On the Mend," *The Ash & Clay* (Los Angeles: Anti Records, 2013), compact disc.

6. William Wordsworth, *The Prelude and Other Poems*, ed. Alexander Gingell and Alessandro Gallenzi (Surrey, UK: Alma Classics, 2019), 108.

7. "Why Is the Sky Blue?" *Nasa Science: SpacePlace*, August 29, 2022, https://spaceplace.nasa.gov.

8. "The Universe," *Space.com*, n.d., https://www.space.com.

9. Geoffrey Chaucer, General Prologue of *The Canterbury Tales*, in *The Complete Poetry and Prose of Geoffrey Chaucer*, ed. John H. Fisher (New York: Holt, Rinehart, and Winston, 1977), 9.

ACKNOWLEDGMENTS

I am grateful to the editors of the publications in which versions of the following chapters first appeared:

bioStories: "Cutting Words"

Foliate Oak: "Impact"

The Phoenix: "Light"

Saint Katherine Review: "God Said"

I am beyond grateful to the readers and judge for the Juniper Prize and to the University of Massachusetts Press for choosing this book to send into the world. I know there were many excellent manuscripts; I am humbled that mine was considered worthy of this honor.

I do not know how to thank my earliest and most faithful readers, who are also my most trusted friends. Annie Kim, Marcia Pelletiere, Jim Rogers: I owe this book to your support, encouragement, gentle prodding, and keen editorial vision. Without your presence in my life, writerly and otherwise, I would not have been able to finish it.

ACKNOWLEDGMENTS

I am grateful to belong to a generous community of writers, graduates of the Warren Wilson College low-residency MFA program, who provide camaraderie, laughter, and a heap of writing advice and inspiration. I am indebted to that entire community; but for this book, in addition to Annie and Marcia, I have reason to thank other members specifically: Michael Jarmer, Anne McCrary Sullivan, and Kristen Staby Rembold, who gave me invaluable feedback on a late draft.

The myth of the writer working alone and isolated in a solitary space is, for me, just that: a myth. I rely on regular interactions with other writers: on their example of showing up to do the work; on their innovations; on their shared experience of life, which often drives them to the writing desk; on their generosity; on their humanity; on their fearlessness in the face of rejection, loss, and the ordinary vicissitudes of life.

My long-time writing group members provide all of that for me and more. That they exist means that I can keep writing. My heartfelt thanks to Kirsten, Marie, Ann, Liz, Rita, Janet, Kathy, and Teresa.

JUNIPER
JUNIPER PRIZE FOR CREATIVE NONFICTION

This volume is the fifth recipient
of the Juniper Prize for Creative Nonfiction,
established in 2018 by the
University of Massachusetts Press
in collaboration with the
UMass Amherst MFA Program
for Poets and Writers, to be
presented annually for an outstanding
work of literary fiction. Like its sister award,
the Juniper Prize for Poetry established
in 1976, the prize is named in honor
of Robert Francis (1901–1987),
who lived for many years at
Fort Juniper, Amherst, Massachusetts.